Not just a
BERKSHIRE FARMER

by Bert Houghton

ISBN 0 9514193 0 7

Front cover illustration by
Mrs Jane Whitaker

Produced through MRM Associates Ltd.
322 Oxford Road, Reading, Berks RG3 1AD

CONTENTS

CONTENTS

FOREWORD

My original purpose in writing these recollections was to inform my children and grandchildren about our family background, my early life, interesting incidents, and about places, customs and other things, which have changed to such an extent in the farming world over the years.

My wife and family have urged me to make my writings available to a wider circle, and the publication of this book is the result.

I trust that the readers will find something of interest even in the passages which are of special concern to members of the family. Since the book is based on memories and notes in my old diaries, may my family and friends forgive any inaccuracies.

I would like to express my thanks to those who have helped me. I am indebted to:

My wife, Ruth, for her continuous encouragement and help in the many hours of painstaking research;

My late Mother, Mrs Lottie Houghton, for providing the family history;

Daughter-in-law, Mrs Grazyna Houghton, assisted by my son, Michael, for typing, preparing and proof-reading the original manuscript;

My son, Antony for help with editing, and the Introduction;

Mrs Jane Whitaker for the illustrations;

And finally my daughter, Mrs Jane Sheppard, Step-Daughter-in-Law, Mrs Maree Fiddler, Mr Jack Perris, a first Cousin, and Miss Dora Jerome, for their contributions.

My Parents

My Parents

The extensive farming enterprise, now run largely by my three sons, Timothy, Richard, and Stephen, owes much to the forethought and hard work of my late parents.

My father and I travelled hundreds of thousands of miles together in various cattle trucks. Usually of the very second-hand variety.

Dealing in livestock we attended many weekly markets – Guildford, Reading, and Newbury, we rarely missed a sale day. We were truly a father and son partnership.

Dad was a kindly man, fair but firm in all his dealings. Calling on local farmers, his opinion would frequently be asked for: "Dew think this weathers gow'n to improve, Frank?" "Alt I to cut my mowing grass?"

Dairy farmers with long experience often said: "Come and have a look at this 'ere cow, see if you thinks hers in calf." This before pregnancy testing by the vet was widespread practice. Anyway Dad's advice was free, the vet had to be paid!!

The cow in question, tied up in the stall was approached on her right side. Dad, his hand clenched, thumb protruding slightly beyond his bent index finger, gently probed the cow's stomach, first one spot, then another, the farmer looking on anxiously. "Yes, she's in calf al'right, here it is, calf's head is knocking my hand right here." says Dad. The farmer trys – without success. "Can't feel a damn thing, still if you says she's in calf, that's good enough for me."

Heifers due with their first calf – Dad could diagnose pregnancy at a very early stage. Drawing out one of her teats, if the spot of fluid was thick and sticky, he'd pronounce her in calf. Old wive's tale, maybe which today's farmers and veterinary surgeons would laugh at. But the fact remains, he was seldom proved wrong.

His skill with sick animals was renowned, his time freely given. When offered payment he would say: "No thanks, that's alright, glad to be of some service, give my son a drink if you want."

July 17th, 1963. My father and I were visiting a farmer at

1

Hermitage, some three miles from home, when without warning, he collapsed and died of a heart attack. He was 79 years old.

I had the traumatic experience of breaking the news to my mother. She bore her loss bravely, a widow for the next twenty-three years. She lived on for her nine grand-children, her daughter Delcie and myself.

She died peacefully on August 20th 1986, after a short illness, in her 90th year.

Both my parents lived full lives, revolving around the farm and the family. They were patient, honest and devoted to each other.

It was through their love and example that I grew up under their guiding influence – a son of the soil.

Born Into Farming

Born in a small whitewashed farmhouse near the village of Beenham. Field Barn Farm lies just off the A4 roughly halfway between the county town of Reading and the market town of Newbury.

The first born of Frank Houghton and his newly married bride, the former Miss Lottie Perris. A weakly child apparently there were times when I wasn't expected to live, but I turned out to be a great survivor and very lucky in many respects. The first grandchild on my mother's side of the family, it would appear that as a small underweight child I was rather spoilt by Grandparents, Aunts and Uncles who travelled far by horse and governess carts to inspect the newborn of Frank and Lottie.

Peace had returned to Europe and the world. The traumatic events of the 1914–18 War had passed like a black cloud leaving in its wake untold thousands of dead and injured.

My father, approaching forty, had registered for military service but had not been called up. The date of my arrival in this beautiful peaceful valley of the Thames was May 9th 1921. Springtime – The green fields of grass and newly sown corn glistening in early morning sunshine would make a pleasant journey for my relatives travelling far by horse drawn transport to see me. I am told that my Mother's younger unmarried sister spent hours jigging me around the room to bring up the 'wind' and stop me squawking my head off. Aunt Dorie has always been my favourite Aunt and still today never forgets to send me a birthday card.

This is my life story, but perhaps I should digress, step back in time to give the reader some of my family background.

My grandparents on my father's side both died before I was born. Farming did not go back for generations on this side. My grandfather, James Mander Houghton was a hosier by trade. He had a shop and also a small factory in Edgebaston, Birmingham where, among other things, he manufactured mortar-board hats for college students. One of his inventions which he patented was the small reinforcing tabs on each corner of the hats to prevent the corners turning up and protect them if thrown down. A seemingly insignificant innovation it helped his business prosper and at one time there were seven Houghton's men's outfitter shops in and around Birmingham. This enterprise continued in the family until the 1960's when they sold out and today the only active member of the old business is Mrs Ivy Houghton of New Friar, Washwater, Newbury.

In 1881 grandfather sold his business interest to a brother and for some unknown reason decided to invest his money in farm land. By now a wealthy city man he purchased what was quite a large farm in those days. Known as Westbrook Old Manor, a lovely English farmhouse, seven thatched cottages and two hundred fertile acres in the beautiful Lambourn valley. Boxford, one of the prettiest villages in Berkshire. What a contrast the family must have felt from the dark, dreary back streets of England's second largest city.

Grandmother had Irish blood and was reputed to have had a vile temper, but grandfather was a placid, even-tempered gentleman of small stature and in later years easily recognised by his white hair and snowy white beard. Unfortunately he did get drunk quite often, then he would fight at the slightest provocation and more often than not had to be carried home protesting loudly that it was not yet closing time.

Grandmother would be waiting, all hell cut loose. He would promise it would never happen again, but it was not until the whole family emigrated to the vast prairies of Canada that his drink problem was finally cured. They had four sons and two daughters and as they grew up it became apparent that the farm couldn't support them all. Even those days some of the little thatched cottages were not required for the farmworkers and grandfather let them for the princely sum of one shilling or one shilling and sixpence per week. These same cottages today (1985) have a price tag of £80,000 each.

With not enough work on the farm, one of his sons, my father, Frank, was apprenticed to a carpenter-wheelwright. One of his first tasks was working in the saw pit, a dirty dusty job usually given to the new boy. A large elm tree would have to be cut into planks for the making of coffins. A workman, standing on top of the horizontal tree, pulled up a huge rip-saw; my father, down below in the pit pulled it back again. Up and down all day, six days a week for three shillings and sixpence. When after three years of learning the trade he

4

asked for a rise, he was given the sack instead (made redundant in todays terms).

These were hard times, just after the turn of the century. My father's brothers were helping their father on the farm. They all wished for their own land but the capital was not available. My father and his family were disgruntled with life in Boxford. There was free land to be had in Canada's wide open spaces, a new life full of adventure and excitement. Much midnight oil must have been burnt as the whole family held serious discussions around the kitchen table. Perhaps a vote was taken before this momentous agreement was reached? They would all emigrate to this 'Promised Land', where each one could get a quarter section, one hundred and sixty virgin acres for the payment of just ten dollars to the Canadian government, providing they farmed and lived on this open prairie for six years. My grandfather didn't wish to go, but it seems he was put under pressure by the rest of his family who wished to get him away from his local pub, because of his drink problem – he was fast becoming an alcoholic.

The fact is they all made the trip across the Atlantic. I have a letter sent back home of the hardships of their journey but unfortunately it is not dated but it must have been sometime between 1906 and 1908. My father farmed on his homestead in Saskatchewan for six years eventually returning before the First World War, dispirited and completely broke. In later years I would listen intensely to his adventures on the homestead.

On my Mother's side farming for a living goes back many generations. My great grandfather, John Perris, farmed at Oakhanger, and was well known as a sheep dealer and always in attendance at the great sheep fairs at East Ilsley. Those great-grandparents of mine had a large family of thirteen children, not unusual in Victorian times, but, unfortunately, only one male child survived, namely my grandfather, also a John Perris, who in his turn farmed and dealt in livestock all his life. A tenant of the Sutton Estate at Hoe Benham, near Stockcross, about six miles from the market town of Newbury. Those grandparents of mine, John and Alice had six children, one of which died in infancy. My mother, born on 28th June 1898, was the eldest of the girls. Christened just plain 'Lottie', she left the village school at Stockcross when she reached fourteen, never going out to work – she helped her mother with the housework, and looked after her younger brothers and sisters. In the summer, she told of assisting with the hay harvest, sitting in a long dress on the hard iron seat of the hayrake collecting the sweet smelling hay in long straight windrows, pitching the crop up and onto the wagons, helping with rick-building then back to the byre to milk the cows. She churned the cream in a big wooden separator, and once a week made the butter for home use and market. The two younger sisters Dorie and Glady, both became school-teachers before their marriages to local men. Of the boys, the eldest of the family, my late Uncle, Jack Perris, served and was badly wounded in the First World War. His younger brother was killed in the conflict. His name was Albert, and it is after him that I am named.

Having recorded my ancestry, let us now return to Field Barn Farm, from where I am told, one lovely sunny morning in the summer of 1921, dressed in a beautiful long gown, I was taken by horse and governess cart, to be christened that afternoon in the tiny Church on the hill at Hoe Benham. Grandparents, aunts, uncles, friends and neighbours also made the pilgrimage to witness the ceremony conducted by the Reverend Patrick Hardy. I cannot say whether I cried during the service, but I did lose a pretty hand knitted shoe on the fifteen mile journey to the church. The family would have stayed the night at Hoe Benham Farm. Drinks flowed to 'wet the baby's head', but I would have been oblivious to these celebrations. The little ivy covered church, no longer used for worship, stands, lonely and sadly neglected nowadays, surrounded by weeds and brambles.

Father continued to farm his fifty acre council holding for the next four or five years. Fifty acres wouldn't give one a living these days, unless they are farmed very intensively. One must appreciate that this land is flat and very fertile with the capacity to grow heavy crops of grass for hay or grazing. Dad didn't grow grain, just an acre or two of roots for cattle feed.

He had his small dairy herd and sold the milk, butter and cream in nearby villages. The Houghton family seemed to have been teat pulling most of this century, why I cannot imagine; one of the messiest of farm animals, which always require feeding and mucking out, not to mention the chore of milking them twice a day, 365 days a year and a good many leap years too. Doing a quick calculation I find some member of our family has called the cows in some 55,000 times! That doesn't take into account the fact that for two years

1981–83, we milked our bovine charges three times a day!!! Some of my family have been sensible enough to find easier ways of making a living.

The reason my parents decided to give up the tenancy of Field Barn Farm so early in their farming career was the fact that my young mother was homesick. It was a thirty mile round trip to visit her parents at Hoe Beenham, not a pleasant journey by horse and trap on winter days with a young child. Pressure was put on Father to try and get a farm nearer her old home.

Dad had made progress during his short occupation of the Beenham holding. He had a good milk round, bought and sold a few cattle and sheep, even purchased a new overtime tractor, much to the amazement of his neighbouring farmers. With this machine, not only did he do his own field work, but did some contract ploughing as well. Dad had a business friend, a certain Mr Larkcom, considered to be an authority on sheep; they struck many a deal over farm yard gates; roving the district by horse and trap, but much time was wasted by the fact that come opening time, Dad (who was almost teetotal) could not get Squire Larkcom past an open pub. "Come on Frank, just a pint and we'll be on our way." But it seems a pint became two, then three, it was seldom short of closing time before a move was made!

Meanwhile my grandmother, Alice Perris, had purchased 41 acres (part of Fishers Farm) for her son Jack, now recovered from his war wounds, he wished to make a start on his own. A small two bedroomed asbestos tiled bungalow was erected on one corner of this land for the total sum of £300, no planning permission had to be obtained in those days.

Now known as 'Briarlea', it is still in the family possession. For some reason when it came to the date for my late Uncle Jack to take over, he changed his mind, staying on in farming with his father. When Jack turned the land down, my Mother seized the opportunity. "We must buy it Frank, the land is cheap and close to home. Think what it means, you'll be a landowner in your own right and not beholding to the whims of county council landlords". It was purchased on the 21st February 1924 for £1329 and ten shillings.

Right or wrong I cannot say, but Dad did purchase this small outlying section of Fishers Farm, the bungalow and the only farm building, an open, south facing, timber-framed, three bay cart shed. Clad in galvanized tin, it served as our cowshed for the next twenty years! Freezing cold in winter, boiling hot in summer, how we withstood those conditions, I'll never know, we must have loved our cows.

Dad signed away the tenancy of Field Barn Farm, moving next Michaelmas, 29th September 1926. The 'goodwill' in the sum of £50 was paid to my father by the new tenant, namely the late Mr 'Bill' Liddiard, founder of the great Berkshire Liddiard farming empire.

This sum did not, of course, include any live or dead farmstock. Everything was moved to the new land now to be called 'Dymond Farm' with the exception of the overtime tractor. With a large mortgage round his neck, Dad couldn't afford this luxury, his shires were moving too, he would revert to 'horse power' on four legs! We didn't own a tractor again until the early days of the Second World War.

School Days

Spring 1926. I was five years old – time for my education to begin. I was to attend Shaw-cum-Donnington Village School, under the strict headmaster Mr Morris. Day one, Dad harnessed 'Dick' our seven year old chestnut gelding, in the shafts of the governess cart, Dick impatiently scraping one iron-shod hoof on the gravel track, all ready to be off. Mum had bought me some new clothes for the occasion. Small, peaked cloth cap, new jacket and of course, short trousers, long thick socks and black boots. A brown leather satchel held a pack of sandwiches, a bottle of home-made lemon drink, and a mac in case of rain. I mounted the step at the rear of the cart, gave Mum a hug and kiss, and couldn't help but notice the tears in her eyes. Dad sat by the little door at the back holding Dick in check with the reins, reins which were looped through two brass rings on the front of the trap then through two more rings on the pad saddle to the horse bridle. Dick wore blinkers yet he rarely shied at anything except on occasions he would swerve alarmingly round a manhole cover in the road. Out onto the main road, we turned south, moving at a swift

trot the beautifully sprung cart swayed gently, the brightly painted wooden wheels had a hard rubber rim which made little sound on the smooth road surface. Dick's shoes beat a regular tattoo as we sped on our way. There was a long whip pointing from its holder on the mudguard, seldom used but there just in case of need. Turning right into Love Lane we fairly raced past other scholars on their way, pulling up at the school gates. A group of children quickly gathered to inspect this new pupil. Hitching Dick to the railings, Dad took me in to see the teacher – there were of course, a few other five year olds starting school on the same day.

One of my parents collected me for the first few weeks of schooling, after that, having made friends with other boys from our direction, I made my own way home. That first day seemed terribly long – I thought it would never end! We didn't really do any lessons for some weeks, just played games and settled in, as our young junior teacher called it. Most of the other children lived close by and went home for lunch, but since I had more than a two mile journey I stayed at school. There was a strange rule that all pupils had to vacate the classrooms during lunch-break, which was from 12 noon till 1.30 PM. Meal service didn't exist at our school, we were left to our own devices. On the edge of the gravel playground there was a row of wooden benches provided for children to sit and eat their sandwiches, if time and distance didn't allow them to return home mid-day. Exposed to the elements with no over-head cover we could hardly be expected to sit there for one and a half hours! Some sympathy was reluctantly shown on frosty winter days, when we were allowed to sit and eat lunch round the classroom coal fire! There was no restriction on leaving the school grounds during lunch break. In fact the teachers seemed to encourage the practice. As the days lengthened with the approach of high summer, I teamed up with two pals who lived nearby. Their names were Bertie Goodman and Albie Raymond. Both country born lads, their main objective in life was to find birds nests, explore keeper-patrolled woods, and fish the River Lambourn with rod, line and worms on bent pins! I'm sure I could count on one hand the times I ate my lunch on the school benches.

I remember my first summer at school – I was often absent due to sickness – colds, sore throat, ear-ache or tummy bug, I was a sickly child. My parents arranged an interview with the headmaster and it was mutually agreed that I attend school half days only through the coming winter. This suited me, I really hated school. The following spring hints were dropped concerning the possible arrival of a new baby. How would you like a brother or sister to play with? I didn't show any great enthusiasm at this prospect, much to the disappointment of my parents. After all, I was quite happy with my two school pals, one couldn't take a young baby climbing trees and birds nesting. It would be sure to get lots of attention, I couldn't see much point in their suggestion, it would completely disrupt the household, babies were such helpless, stupid objects.

'Mummy's gone away for a short holiday" I was told. I thought this very strange, most odd, she had never done that before. As compensation my Auntie Dorie came to look after Dad and so things at home went on as normal; better in fact. My aunt cooked the breakfast eggs much nicer, fussing over me whilst I got ready for school. "Have you had enough to eat, Bertie. Got your lunch? Don't forget to put your mac on if it rains on the way back from school – mustn't have you catching cold with your Mum away." On April 4th 1927, there was great excitement when I came down for breakfast. "You've got a baby sister!" Dad explained; Aunt Dorie couldn't stop talking, seemed to be laughing and crying at the same time. 'Good job its all over Frank. It's been a long night, you must be pleased though, and its a girl, just what you both wanted ... What are you going to call her, or haven't you yet decided?" I just couldn't comprehend why a new baby should cause such excitement. "You will not be going to school today." Dad announced. "Oh good news." I thought to myself "This baby has brought one blessing if nothing else!"

Born at a private nursing home in London Road, Newbury, my new sister was to be called Delcie May.

I was not allowed to visit, young children didn't enter such mysterious establishments. Sex, birth and death were taboo, not to be discussed in front of the young. It was explained to me at great length that Mummy had found the new baby under a gooseberry bush. I remember thinking, "Ten days seems an awful long time to be looking, must have been difficult to find, I must say!"

"I'm going to fetch Mummy and your new sister back today" said Dad, "Would you like to come too?" Auntie Dorie will be staying with us for a few more days. The horse was harnessed into the governess cart, looking extra spick and span, Dad dressed in a suit, ("must be something special, this baby") he seldom got poshed up

11

like that, he'd even cleaned his shoes! Pulling up sharply at the nursing home, Dick was hitched to the iron railings. I was told to sit still and be quiet, while Dad mounted the steps to the front door two at a time. He was inside for some time, I was getting impatient, Dick had been quietly nibbling the well-trimmed privet hedge, now he pricked up his ears as the large door of the maternity home swung open. The matron, a buxom figure, was guiding my Mother out and down the steps. Mum grasping her precious bundle of humanity. Dad, looking anxious, followed down the path through the wooden gate round to the rear of the trap. Opening the door he said, "Steady does it" as he helped Mum aboard.

Safely on the rugged bench seat, Mum pulled the shawl aside, "Well, Bertie, what do you think of your little sister?" she inquired. I peeped inside: "Isn't she tiny!" I explained as I stared down at a miniscule pink round face no larger than an orange. Her eyes were clamped shut, and she was frowning crossly. "What a funny squashed nose she'd got" I thought to myself. Aloud "Alright I suppose" without much enthusiasm. Dad has to unhitch the horse, quickly get in and grasp the reins, and we swung round to the right across the street, heading for home. That chestnut cob of Dads was a good mover, and always faster on a return trip, he knew when he was going home. It was not many minutes before we turned into our gravelled farm track and stopped outside the house. Dick's sweat lathered flanks heaving like bellows.

Our little household was never the same again. Mum gave such a lot of her time and affection to her new charge. Feeding times were every three or four hours. Nappy changing was another unpleasant chore. "Here you are Bertie, hold your little sister for a minute whilst I put her milk on to warm." She was often wet anyway!

I was not to be blessed with any more brothers or sisters, and to be fair, I did grow to be quite fond of my sister. She grew up to be a happy, jolly person and we had great fun together.

Village School Life

Boys and girls played together in a large playground. On one side was a long row of wooden seats fixed to the ground. This seating arrangement divided the play area from small vegetable plots in which boys were taught the fundamentals of gardening. I always enjoyed those afternoon periods when our time was devoted to digging, planting seeds and weeding. To watch the results of our labour as seedlings pricked through the soil. Then came the harvest of our produce, much of which was given to elderly people in the village.

At the far end of our playground were a row of eight bucket lavatories. Four for the girls and four for the boys separated by sheets of corrugated tin. The boys used to tease and frighten the girls in all sorts of ways. I recall one occasion when myself and three of my mischievous 'friends' found a large toad. When the coast was clear, Albie Raymond, a nimble lad, dashed into the girl's toilet placing our 'find' in a newly emptied bucket. We now retreated to a quiet corner, waiting for the first girl to go in. It so happened that our victim was a timid girl, fairly new to the school, and quite unprepared for our devilment. She evidently saw or heard the frog-like animal as she prepared to sit on the seat.

There was a strong country supersitition held by us children that toads spat fire and were to be avoided at all costs. Not surprising therefore that the poor child stampeded out, screaming, with her lace-edged knickers hanging round her knees! Then they fell to her ankles and she pitched headlong into a dirty rain puddle. Our fun was short lived. The whole story came out. Next day all four of us were up before Mr Morris, our headmaster. We received a severe reprimand. A most repugnant prank he called it. In addition we all had to lean over a desk and take six strokes of the cane on our backsides!!

At our school one could catch head-lice quicker than measles and my Mother, a spotlessly clean person, dreaded the time when my

sister or I might be sent home by 'Nitty Nancy' as we children called the health nurse.

Once or twice each term 'Nitty Nancy' called at our school to examine our heads. On entering our class-room teacher would say: "Heads down children." We were expected to fold our arms across the desks and rest our heads on them. The nurse slowly made her way round the class peering and probing each dirty, untidy mop in turn. Every so often the nurse would ask a child's name, entering it in a little note book, most humiliating for the child concerned. Next nurse and teacher held a whispered conversation, before asking the affected children to step out to the front of the class. Each would then be sent home with a note to their parents instructing them how to deal with the parasites; they would also get a home visit from the nurse.

I was often found to be 'cooty' more likely due to the company I kept rather than the state of my home. My Mother would sit me at the kitchen table, my head held low over a newspaper whilst she ran a very small-toothed comb through my hair. The lice fell out onto the paper and we killed them by squashing each one with our thumb-nail, leaving just a splash of blood – my blood of course!

The comb failed to remove the nits (eggs of the louse) which cling in strings to a strand of ones hair, only to hatch out in a few more days time to re-infest the victim once again.

Even in writing this sorry story, thinking once again of 'Nitty Nancy' it makes me want to scratch my head!!

Schoolboy Escapades

Perhaps my particular school friends were a bad influence on me, but I don't think I was the ringleader in our mischievous adventures. As we grew older our lunch-breaks found us venturing further and further afield. With no watch between us, we had little track of time, often returning to school after the bell only to play truant for the rest of the afternoon. Tomorrow was a long way off, there were some jolly interesting places to visit, turning our backs on the school, kicking stones before us as we retraced our steps. I had the cane more than once for being absent without a written excuse. Down Love Lane, left at the road junction, just past Donnington Priory to the humped-backed bridge, the three of us climbed a wooden fence to follow the north bank of the river as it twisted its course through low-lying water meadows. In a quiet backwater there is a small island. Ten or twelve feet of deep fast-flowing water prevented three would-be explorers. We had pondered over the problem of getting across on many previous occasions, but the current was far too deep and fast for wading. A springtime gale had brought down a dead ash tree up-stream. After much strenuous levering with long poles we succeeded in floating it down river to make a precarious bridge to our island. I cannot remember discovering anything of great significance apart from one or two abandoned birds nests, but it gave us three boys a great thrill to tread "where no man had trod before".

Autumn, the time for fruit, we knew of half a dozen lovely apple orchards which could be raided. Knowledge of holes in hedge or fence, days of the week when the gardener was absent, or time of his dinner break were all essential to a successful scrumping. Growing by the side of St. Marys Church were several ancient yew trees, entwined with ivy and creeping vines. Little sunlight ever penetrated through the tangled canopy overhead. Called the Wilderness we had wonderful games in its dark depths, and it made a marvellous hide away if chased by bad tempered Shaw House gardeners!

Homeward bound in summertime there is a short cut through Shaw Dene and the woods behind, but that didn't mean we arrived home any earlier. Mainly undisturbed, those quiet woodlands hid many nesting birds. Avid egg collectors we spent hours searching thick undergrowth for the elusive nightingale, linnet or blackcap's cleverly camouflaged nest. The robin built in the oddest of places and there was always the chance that we would discover a cuckoo's egg in some unsuspecting bird's nest. Why should a large bird like the cuckoo lay its unwelcome egg in small bird's nests, how it could sit on such a small platform I never really found out.

Ponds were interesting places covered in algae or 'ginny-green-teeth' as we used to call it, the dark still water was home to multitudes of frogs, tadpoles and brightly coloured newts and lizards all of which could be caught by dangling a large jam jar on a length of string and yank smartly upwards at the correct moment. Our catch, proudly taken home to reside on the porch shelf, fed on the most inappropriate food until my mother finally said, "Take those poor creatures back where you got them from – I don't want them here another day." Our captives were not always released in the same water, we assumed they would be just as happy in some new pond.

Homeward bound one late July afternoon my companions Bertie, Albie and on this occasion young George Scaplehorn, penetrated much deeper into the oak woodland of Brick Kiln wood, in a clearing we discovered a large wiremesh pen. Six feet high with wooden stakes every few yards, it enclosed thick stands of rhododendron shrubs, a small galvanized tin shelter some two feet high under which half-grown pheasants were feeding. There seemed to be hundreds of them and as we watched many of the birds would pace continuously round the pen, poking their heads through the two inch mesh. "That's cruel, keeping birds shut up in a pen like that" said Albie. "If they don't like it in there why don't they fly out then, they've got wings" I queried. "Cos they haven't learnt how to use 'em proper yet, that's why" someone else explained. Four boys discussing the pros and cons of keeping pheasants in release pens to provide sport for some rich man's gun later in the season.

"Let's open the gate and let 'em out, they will be much happier with the whole wood to roam in" I said. "Wot about the foxes, they'll eat them" Bertie said. "Course they won't, pheasants jump up on branches, and go to roost in the trees" I countered. Unanimously agreed, the latch was lifted, the gate opened inwards, we retreated to thick undergrowth to watch developments. Some pheasants making their way round came up against the gate, couldn't find a way round

this obstacle, only to retreat the other way again. It wasn't long before one, two, then many more birds found freedom. They quickly vanished into brambles and bracken. Making our way home we all agreed we had done the right thing. Nevertheless we thought it would be prudent to avoid those woods for a few weeks!

I recall one more adventure of my school days which nearly ended in disaster. The last day of school before breaking up for the Christmas holidays, the weather was bitterly cold, it had been freezing hard for many days. Hoare frost glistened on bare tree branches, many small birds that had hatched despite our egg stealing

18

would not survive this winter. That evening our school play was to be presented in front of admiring parents. For my part I was one of the ten little nigger boys.

Opposite Shaw Church where there are now playing fields was a large pond, the water quite deep in places. Warned not to play in that area, this only made it more attractive to us. Signs on trees saying "Private Woods – Trespassers will be prosecuted" always made entry more dangerous and daring, the excitement of the chase that much greater. During our lunch break, Albie, Bertie and myself made our way to the frozen pond. Carefully we tested the ice by jumping on the edge. "Yes, its strong enough, look how thick it is" Albie said, peering down at the black water beneath. Taking long runs from the bank we would hurl ourselves across the smooth ice ignoring the occasional ominous crack. The game had progressed for sometime, when suddenly, without warning, in the deepest part of the pond, the ice broke and I vanished through the hole. Now, I have learnt since that if one falls through ice the chances of surviving are slim because one cannot find the hole in the ice again. Following the shock of the ice cold water, I remember going right to the bottom before striking upwards. I could swim, but of course had winter clothing on, plus heavy boots, and I couldn't find the hole in the ice! I owe my life to my two staunch friends, Albie and Bertie. They had found a long forked branch which they pushed through the hole in the ice from a safe spot near a willow tree. By good fortune I clutched this moving branch which guided me to where I had fallen through. Holding this life-line my pals pulled me out. I'd almost had it, and chilled to the marrow, I gasped for breath, blurting out my thanks, whilst shivering on the bank. Showing deep concern, my two friends took off some of my wet clothes, tried to wring out the icy water, but I had to put the same coat and trousers back on again. "You had better get off home, Bert, you cannot go back to school like that". "Course I am, and thanks for pulling me out" I replied. I've never got home so quickly before. Mum was most concerned, giving me a hot bath, hot drink and dry clothes, I soon recovered. Determination made me return that same evening to take my place in the school play. Before the curtain rose our headmaster issued a grave warning to all the school children and their parents about the dangers of youngsters playing near water. He also announced that Bert Houghton, foolishly sliding on thin ice, had fallen through, but for the quick action taken by two members of the class the ten little nigger boys almost became nine.

"Let that be a lesson to you all!" With that, the curtain was pulled to one side, our much rehearsed performance got underway.

Christmas holidays over, a new term commenced. We never took any exams at our school except for a scripture exam in which I came second in the class which doesn't say much for the other pupils! My best subject was arithmetic. Good at figures, I loved doing sums, learning my tables and solving mathematical problems. History held a certain fascination but I couldn't remember important dates. "1066" the Battle of Hastings was one of the few and that possibly because us boys regretted the fact that "poor ole 'arold was darn unlucky getting an arrow stuck in his eye". We did have a good sports field, in low-lying ground between the Castle Pub and Donnington Castle. I played in the second football team, often as their goal-keeper until on one occasion my thumb was dislocated saving a particularly fine penalty shot. Also in the cricket team, but I was never fond of the sport, I found it rather slow. By the time I reached my twelfth birthday, I had not advanced far academically. My parents, anxious for me to receive a 'better education' put my name down for entry into Newbury Grammar School. I put up opposition to this plan, making the excuse that it would be much farther to travel each day, and I didn't wish to desert my school friends of long standing. Foolishly my parents capitulated. In hindsight, I now regret that decision. In later years all of my seven children attended this secondary modern school, and received a far better education leading to university reading.

To the Rescue

I have no recollection of living at Beenham, and only hazy memories of life at the little bungalow. My sister, Delcie, wasn't born at that time, there is six years between us. One incident I do remember and that was the time when I 'helped' in the making of an iron gate. Dad had a fierce fire going to heat the metal rods he was using. Of course I had to catch hold of one didn't I? The skin was burnt from the palm of my right hand. There must have been a panic to get the horse harnessed up and hitched in the trap to rush me to hospital for treatment.

My sister at the age of three had a great love of animals. Every day she would be outside feeding poultry or perhaps some of the pigs, which seemed to roam freely around the farm. On this particular day, Dad was in the big tin cowshed, milking his cows. The shorthorn bull we had at that time was patiently waiting, chewing the cud, until he could lead the herd out to pasture.

Delcie, probably looking for her father, wandered out into the field with the bull. More in play than in anger, he knocked her over, and was pushing her around with his horns like a rag doll, when I heard

22

her cry out. As I raced across the meadow and over the fence, my one thought was to save my little sister. When the bull saw me, he was undecided what to do with this new intrusion. He stared at me with his beady eyes, at the same time pawing the ground angrily with his hoof. Reaching out, I grabbed Delcie's hand, and half dragged, half carried her to the fence.

The bull was sent for slaughter the very next day, a pity really, as it had up till then been a docile animal, and I'm sure it hadn't meant any harm. "If you must have a bull on the farm, you'll have to build a stout pen, and keep it under control," insisted my Mother, "With young children around, one of them will get killed next time."

Dad never did build a bull pen – the replacement bull wandered freely round with the herd all year round, letting nature take its own course.

A Train Journey

From an early age, I loved to travel, especially train journeys.

My aunt and uncle lived at Wingfield, near Trowbridge. Uncle Sid (Mr Maber) was a head game keeper on a large estate. I had made one previous visit with my parents, and although I was only nine years old, I pestered Dad and Mum to let me go on my own for the summer holidays. They expressed doubts about my safety on such a long journey. However, at the end of the Summer Term, July 1930, my case was packed.

Dad and Mum took me by horse and trap to the 'down line' of Newbury Station. Waiting for the London–Penzance Express, a slip of a lad in my summer gear, sandals, long woollen socks, short grey flannel trousers, bare-kneed, I had a label fastened to my brown jacket, giving my intended destination. As is my nature, I was quite calm and relaxed, Dad was always very placid too, but Mum was quite jittery at the prospect of her son going away from home for the first time. A distant whistle signalled the approaching train. By now the platform was crowded with fellow passengers, business men in trilby hats, commercial travellers, families with children going off for the week-end, working men going to the next big town, the odd peace-time soldier or airman going home on leave. Round the curve of the double track line came the massive locomotive, black smoke from the chimney blown back over the long line of pullman coaches. The driver had been slowing his great engine down for the last mile, measuring the distance to perfection he finally halted with the coaches alongside the platform. This was the days of the Great Western Railway at its best.

The doors opened, we had to wait whilst other passengers got off before Dad could put my luggage on board, Mum kissed me good-bye, "Now be a good boy, and do as Auntie Dorie tells you, we'll collect you when you come back, just send us a postcard with the time of the train." I was put in charge of the guard, and told whatever I did "Don't lose your ticket or your money. Uncle Sid will meet you at Trowbridge Station, have a nice time. Bye-bye." The

uniformed guard was now walking the length of the train, slamming the heavy doors shut as he passed, at the same time announcing in a clear voice, "Next stop Westbury, next stop Westbury. This train stops at Taunton, Exeter, Plymouth, Penzance." I knew that I had to change at Westbury, the guard had promised to hand me over to the guard of the local Trowbridge train. Our guard had now reached his brake van at the rear of the carriages, door open, ready to alight, he gave a mighty blast on his whistle at the same time waving the green flag to the engine driver leaning out over the foot plate of his locomotive.

We were moving, the great wheels of the engine up front turning very slowly. Steam under pressure hissed out from its innards. I waved from the carriage window, as I realised that Mum and Dad were being left behind. Up front the fireman, perhaps stripped to the waist, shovelled coal from the tender into the open furnace under the boiler. The driver, black and greasy, but very experienced, would be checking his pressure gauges, turning wheels and watching signals ahead.

Far from being nervous, or lonely, I enjoyed every minute of my first long train journey. I still find delight in travelling by rail, having in later life crossed vast distances in far flung areas of the world.

With a full head of steam, we quickly gathered speed, how exciting it was to race non-stop through Kintbury, Hungerford, and Great Bedwyn stations. People waiting with their children to see the express flash past, and I was travelling on it!!

Rushing through the green countryside, the clickety-click, clickety-click, clickety-click of the wheels passing over rail expansion gaps made a pleasurable rhythm.

It didn't seem that long before I realised we were slowing down, looking out of my carriage window as we pulled into a station, I read the name 'Westbury' on the sign post. Finally coming to a halt the great locomotive belched smoke and steam, seemed to be almost panting with exertion like a race horse after a record breaking run. A GWR porter was shouting "Westbury, change here for Trowbridge, Bradford-on-Avon, Bath." People were gathering their luggage before getting off. I kept a tight grip on my solitary case as I stepped down to the platform. What a hive of activity. Someone gave a shout as they recognised a face in the crowd, a child crying having momentarily lost its parents, business men pushing and shoving, porters carrying luggage, a lady with a very small dog on a lead. "Mind your backs please" bawled a porter pushing a line of little trucks stacked high with mail and parcels. The crowds quickly thinned, I was beginning to wonder what to do next when my kind guard spotted me: "Come on young man, this way." We headed for a small waiting room; inside, I was handed over to an elderly porter: "Make sure this youngster gets on the next train for Trowbridge, George." With that, my escort was on his way to slam shut more doors, blow his whistle, and wave his green flag once more.

The local train went at a much more leisurely speed, it was but a short journey of only some eight or ten miles. Getting off at Trowbridge station, my uncle was waiting for me. "Well done, young Bert, you've made it!" Picking up my case, he said: "We are going to walk out to the main street and catch a bus to Wingfield, Auntie Dorie is cooking some supper for us." The local bus, an ancient Ford, with five or six ladies returning from the shops, chugged unhurriedly through the country lanes of Somerset. "Nearly there now, there's our house just ahead" said Uncle Sid. Sure enough there was my Aunt waiting at the cottage door, all smiles. "Hello Bert, how nice to see you." She gave me a big kiss. I didn't like fussy ladies kissing me, but there, what can you do about it. They soon got tired of the habit if you screwed your face up as though it was painful. "I've got a nice supper ready for you, I expect you're hungry after your long journey?"

It was explained to me that the cottage was extremely small, and since they didn't have a single bed, I would be sleeping in the bath. "I hope you don't mind Bert" said Aunt Dorie apologetically. "No, no, of course not" I replied. "But won't you or Uncle Sid want to have a bath?" I said. "No, we can manage, we're too busy in the summer time anyway. Uncle Sid has got a lot of work to do this time of year with his pheasants." I spent many summer vacations at the keeper's cottage, and never once did I sleep in a bed!

Game Keeper's Assistant

It was during my annual summer visits to Wingfield that I was to gain much knowledge about pheasant-rearing, plus an insight into a keeper's job, in particular the skills needed to trap or shoot vermin. To someone whose task was to rear game-birds any creature that preyed on pheasant eggs or young chicks was ruthlessly destroyed.

Pheasant chicks were hatched from eggs on the premises, not purchased as poults from large hatchers. There was much more work involved in the preparation of the bird's food than there is today. I became very interested in the rearing of game birds and my uncle seemed to appreciate my assistance. "Come down next Easter Holidays, I can find plenty of jobs for you to do" he said. Next Easter, almost twelve years old, I did my train journey once more, arriving in time to search the woods and undergrowth for pheasant nests. If you take the fertile eggs and place them under a broody hen, the eggs and young chicks are much safer from predators; and the hen pheasant will soon lay another clutch of eggs. All this results in far greater numbers of poults reaching maturity. Broody hens were purchased in great numbers from local farmers, always willing to part with their old birds for a good price. Economically they were not worth keeping around another season for egg production anyway.

"You had better get to bed, young Bert" my aunt said after supper. Forgetting that I was still sleeping in the bath! We made an early start next morning, there was white frost on the grass as we left the keepers cottage just as it was getting light. Uncle Sid went across the yard to the kennels, opening one of the gates, he let out Marcus, his young black retriever. The other dogs made a real rumpus at being left behind, barking and jumping up on their hind legs, pleading to be allowed to be let out.

"Go and get the twelve bore, Bert, it's in the gun room, it will not be loaded". "Bring a few cartridges too, we may see a fox or a stray cat at this time of the day." I hurried to do his bidding. This was a better life than school days, I resolved that I would become a gamekeeper when I was fourteen. Marcus like the other dogs was

28

well trained and kept to heel, Uncle and I crossed the lane, over the stile, we now made our way, following a well worn foot-path to the wicket gate on the far side of the meadow. Our way led us through a leafy track into the depth of the wood. The sun rising in the east was casting shafts of sunlight through the upper branches of the great oak trees. Suddenly we emerged into a long wide drive, beneath the overhanging branches were row upon row of hen coops, each containing a broody hen sitting on fourteen to sixteen fertile pheasant eggs. An old shepherd's hut served as a food store. Standing on four massive iron wheels it was rat proof, provided the little step ladder was shut inside at night. Close by was another large tin shed, this contained all the paraphernalia of the game keeper. Everything likely to be required for the rearing of pheasants to the destruction of their predators. I loved to ferret around looking at all the snares, cages and traps of every description. All had their use and over the years I was taught the skill of setting them, cleverly camouflaged to catch unsuspecting creatures. Stoats, weasels and grey squirrels could be caught by placing a gin trap, well hidden under an old horse-shoe tile drain placed by a tree or in a dry ditch. Owls, jays, magpies, kestrels etc. fell to a baited trap set on a top of a stout pole often erected in some small clearing in the woods. On shoot days the squire and his friends judged the merits of the gamekeeper by the number of well shown high birds put over the guns, and the rows of decayed bodies hanging by their necks or rat-like claws swinging slowly in the wind. Beautiful, innocent, inhabitants of the forest, doomed to be shot or destroyed on sight for no other reason than their preference for the odd pheasant egg or chick.

The sun was now well up. A fine day once the frost had cleared. Our first task was to set the broody hens out for their daily feed and exercise. Beside each coop was a cord attached to a wooden stake driven into the ground. The top of each coop had a sliding panel. Opened, it revealed a Rhode Island Red or White Sussex, wings expanded, feathers extended to cover her clutch of pheasant eggs. She would cluck angrily, pecking at the hand which sought to remove her. I had a thick pair of gloves which I wore for protection whilst lifting the bird out to be fastened by one leg, beside her coop. We worked quickly down the line, the birds had fifteen minutes to eat their rations before being carefully replaced for their next twenty-four hour vigil. Eggs had to be turned, broken ones removed, occasionally a hen would go off being broody, stand up, allowing the eggs to get cold with the resulting loss of perhaps fifteen nice chicks. She received no mercy, no second chance, she was due for the pot, we had a lot of chicken dinners during the hatching season! Twenty-one days the hens sat patiently on the eggs, during this time the chick had formed, now it had to break out first by pecking a small hole in the shell until finally it broke apart. It was great to lift off the hens, and find a crowd of baby chicks, it is amazing how quickly they dry after leaving the broken shell and peep out from beneath the hen's wing feathers.

"There's one here that can't get out, Uncle Sid, shall I help it?" I enquired. "No, don't do that, if it can't get out itself, it will never be any good, always weakly, let it be" was his answer.

A small run made of fine meshed galvanized wire on a light timber frame was placed in front of each coop. The chicks could enter this run through the vertical wooden bars of the coop, placed too close together for the foster mother to follow her adopted family. Their first feed would be chopped hard boiled eggs mixed with bread crumbs. One of my jobs was to prepare this mixture and help to feed and water our new charges. Two pound jam jars half-filled with clean water were placed upside down on a small plate. The air in the jar allows just a small quantity of water for the chicks to drink. Given a larger container, they would probably drown themselves. The chicks grow quickly being fed on boiled maize, chat potatoes and other scraps cooked in big coppers. Some of the ingredients of this concoction were known only to my Uncle, passed on to him from his father, who was also a gamekeeper. One of my tasks was to keep the copper fire going from the stock of sawn logs stored in a lean-to close by. This mysterious mixture, bubbling away had to be stirred frequently with a large stick. It smelled quite appetizing!

At eight weeks, the hens were removed, and the chicks, now larger than adult blackbirds, were placed in large wire pens deeper in the wood. These 'release pens' were the birds' home for a few weeks until they had learnt to roost on tree branches in the pens. Next, they were let out with the freedom of the whole wood, but if fed regularly each day, they did not stray far. It was a great sight at feeding time, calling the birds with a special whistle. They suddenly appeared from the undergrowth and collected in a long wide clearing, hundreds of plump young pheasants, the smart cock birds in their brightly coloured plumage, all eager to feed on a diet of cracked wheat or tailings, and kibbled maize.

This would be the routine, until one cold winter's day a few months later, when a long line of beaters, assisted by hard-working dogs, drove the well-grown birds up, to fly with the wind in their tails over the tops of the highest oak and beech trees, out and clear over the waiting guns. Each man had two guns, a pair of Purdeys or Holland & Holland, expensive weapons made by the finest English Craftsmen. A 'loader' kept the second gun loaded to hand over when the first gun was fired. Some crack shots claim to have two, three or more dead birds falling out of the sky at any one time if the birds were flying thick and fast. I must admit it rather saddened me to witness the broken, lead-shattered bodies blasted out of the sky, retrieved to their masters by well-trained gun dogs, all in the name of sport.

My First Girl Friend

Whilst on those annual summer holidays to Wingfield the friendly village postman took me on his rounds in his red delivery van, which was very much against the company rules – he would drop me off as we passed his house. I could then play with his daughter, Norwyn, who was my age – about 10 years. I have a photo of myself sitting sedately in the garden of their home, enjoying afternoon tea. Back home I would have been ridiculed by my male school pals for having tea with a silly girl, of course! Her father took me to places of great interest in and around Trowbridge; the factories making broadcloth, a local industry since the fourteenth century; the printing works producing the local newspapers. I was most impressed by the speed with which they came off the press. The type had to be set by hand, a laborious process. On another occasion I rode on the footplate of a giant locomotive some five miles to the next station – we had no coaches with us – we were going to hitch up to a line of goods wagons.

My second summer holiday in the West Country over, I returned home. I was due back to school in a few days, when a letter addressed to my parents arrived from my aunt with the news that Norwyn had gone down with diphtheria. She is very ill, I'm afraid, you must watch Bert's health carefully for the next few days, he spent a lot of time at her home recently!" My parents were always of the opinion that if any illness was going round I was sure to catch it. This time was no exception, and a few days later I awoke with a very high temperature, inflammation of the throat, and soon was quite ill. The doctor was called for only to confirm Mum and Dad's fears. In those days diphtheria was often fatal to young children. I would have to be moved to hospital immediately. My Mother insisted on nursing me herself. Our doctor said that decision would be made by the district health inspector, who'd be calling shortly at our house. When he came next day he stressed that I had to stay in the same bedroom, not come downstairs under any circumstancse, and my Father must not sell milk or dairy products until the 'all clear' was given. This last rule was quite a set-back to a farmer who made his living by selling fresh milk.

Each day I grew weaker, I was really dreadfully ill. Later, I was told that the doctor held out faint hopes of my recovery. When the crisis of my illness was reached, he said "If he is still alive in the morning, I think he may pull through." I did just that, but tragically, Norwyn, died.

During convalescence I was allowed to sit outside in the garden, but on doctor's instructions forbidden to use the stairs in the house. So the rick ladder had to be positioned against the window-sill, and for some weeks the rather unusual sight of a small boy dressed in his pyjamas, covered by a heavy dressing gown could be seen climbing a ladder back into his bedroom!

I am positive that it was only my mother's devoted nursing that saved my life.

33

Pepper on the Cabbages

Now that we had moved from Beenham to Dymond Farm, my parents made frequent visits to my Grandparents' Farm at Hoe Benham. Not possessing a brother, I found my cousin Jack Perris, nine months my junior, good company. At ten years of age, we were affectionately described as a 'couple of young rascals.' It would be difficult to say which was the most mischievous.

It was customary to send us two boys to Sunday School, something we detested, for one thing it meant dressing in our Sunday best. More than once we had been in trouble going off birds' nesting and such activities on our way back from Church. I recall this particular Sunday morning. It was a damp, dreary, overcast day, with intermittent showers of light rain. Jack and I had hoped that the inclement weather would prevent us being sent to Sunday School, but it was not a long walk to the little Church, and I presume our respective parents had hopes that the lessons would help us spiritually, and perhaps improve our behaviour!

Dressed in our best Sunday suits, myself wearing for the first time a new mackintosh, we kicked stones up the road and played other games such as trying to jump over the biggest water puddles without landing with a splash in the middle, until hearing the bell ringing, we had to run the last few hundred yards to get to the Church on time. After a dreary hour, mainly spent passing some sweets around, and carving figures on the seats with two bent nails we had found in our pockets, class was closed. None the wiser for all the efforts of the dedicated teachers, we made our way homewards. Knowing that if we went back into the farmhouse, we should be told to "Sit still you two, till dinner time. Read a book or something."

We wandered around the farmyard but there was little there that interested us. If we played with the water in the cattle trough, someone would look out of a window and put a stop to innocent games. There was still an hour to while away before lunch. For some reason we followed the little path that led to the big kitchen garden at the rear of the house.

34

Now Grandad Perris, having a large family to support, was a keen gardener. Never a weed to be seen, the grass paths and hedges always well-trimmed, and this Summer it looked a picture of perfection. He had a prize-winning patch of savoy cabbages, just about ready for harvest. We were making our way up the centre garden path when Jack said: "Look, Bert, there's a bag of soot." I glanced at it without much interest. Jack spoke again, saying: "Grandad puts soot on his cabbages, that's why he always grows such whoppers and wins prizes with them too!" I was not really convinced of the logic of this statement, but then Jack was always so much more knowledgeable than myself, perhaps he was right, not worth having a fight over, so I accepted his word.

"Well," I replied, "if that's the case, why don't we put some soot on them, it will save Grandad a job and he'll be pleased with us." I opened the bag of soot, putting my hands in and bringing out a double handful, sprinkling some of this lovely black stuff on the nearest cabbage. "Not like that, silly," says Jack, "you've got to cut them in half first, then put the soot inside, otherwise it will not make them grow. Let's find something to cut them with."

He makes his way to the little garden shed at the end of the path, disappears inside, a few seconds later, comes running back waving a spade triumphantly. "This should do the job," he exclaims. Raising the weapon high above his head, he brings it round in a wide sweep, like a Viking Warrior using his battle axe. He sliced the first savoy in half as neat as could be. "Now put a good dose of soot on that one." Jack orders me. The spade goes up and round again with lightening speed, but this time he missed, cut the cabbage off at the root. I give a gasp, "Watch out!! you big nit, you nearly took my 'ead off that time." "Well, keep back out of my way then, I've got to cut 'em first." Jack returns to his task, up and round swings the spade as expertly the prize cabbages are beheaded. Prudently I give Cousin Jack a wide berth, as he moves up each neat row of savoys still swinging the spade.

Realising I'm not keeping up on the peppering, travelling back-wards and forwards to the soot bag, just taking a handful at a time, Jack says: "Find a tin or something." Looking around I find an old saucepan under the hedge, "Just the thing, now I can speed the job up, keep pace with the slicing!" I think to myself. Jack, well fed and a bit on the chubby side, is out of breath, and leans on his spade. "This is hard work, you have a go, Bert, I'll do the sooting." He reaches for

the saucepan, but I hold on. "No, I want to do this," I replied. The next minute we are rolling on the rainwashed, muddy garden, fighting for possession of the saucepan. Jack wins control instantly turning it upside down on my head, my cap was knocked off in the melee, and the rain which was coming down heavily, washes the soot over my eyes, ears, nose and down my neck. Not to be outdone in the conflict, I grab a double handful from the sack, and slap it on Jack's head. Things were really warming up. At that moment, we heard a distant call: "Dinner time, where have you two boys got to?" It was the deep voice of Grandad, calling from the front door.

Only then, on standing back, breathing heavily from the exertion of the struggle which had just taken place, did we get the chance to look at each other. It was then we realised the dreadful state we were both in. "Golly," said Jack, "you're covered in soot! All on your new mac too!" "You're no better," I replied, "we shan't half cop it, twas your fault, you started the silly game, Jack!" "No, it wasn't me, you were just as bad." "Still, I 'spect Grandad will be pleased we've peppered his cabbages" I pointed out hopefully.

Following the appetizing smell of roast beef and baked potatoes, we slowly made our way to the front door. Standing there on the doorstep, looking most dejected, two of the dirtiest 'young rascals' imaginable. Our Sunday best covered in soil, soot and wet with the rain. From the kitchen, where Sunday lunch had been carefully laid out on the beautiful, old pine-topped table, came unbelieving gasps of astonishment. Then silence, until our elders all started to talk at once. We didn't known whether to stand our ground, or run away for ever! But we seemed to be rooted to the spot, in a state of shock. The next thing I remember, is Jack and I being dragged off to the bathroom, made to take off all our clothes, being immersed in water that was none too warm, and scrubbed until we turned a bright pink colour.

Dressed again in some makeshift clothes we did eventually get a late lunch. Our best suits and my new mac never came clean again, and I believe they were burnt. My pocket money was stopped for six months. When Grandad saw his cabbages, his reaction was very much the opposite to our expectations, and we were banned from his vegetable garden for life!!

Another Escapade

Almost a year had passed since the escapade over the peppering of the cabbages. Whilst the prank certainly had not been forgotten, Jack and I maintained a low profile when in Grandad's presence. The kitchen garden was still strictly out of bounds.

The following Spring, whilst on another weekend visit to Hoe Benham Farm, Jack and I were searching the back of the brickwall at the entrance to the farm-yard. We were looking for nests of the Great Tit, which love to build in any small cavity in a wall or hole in a tree.

We had seen a Great Tit hopping amongst the branches of a blackthorn. Probably the cockbird, but we couldn't be certain because the sexes are alike in plumage. It was never still, hanging head downwards to inspect a bud, seeking insects or seeds, hammering away with its powerful little beak.

Finding a loose brick with signs that a hole was used by a small bird, it was mutually agreed that there must be a nest there with a good chance of eggs. Neither of us had as yet obtained an egg from this colourful little British resident, so something just had to be done about it. There was no way we could get our hand into such a small space. This time I took the initiative by saying: "We will have to get tools of some kind to remove a brick or two, we can soon replace them when we get the eggs out. Go and get a hammer and chisel from Grandad's workshop." "No, you go, it was your idea!" Jack replies.

I jumped over the wall, stealthily making my way through the shrubs of the flower garden, darting from cover to cover, I make the workshop undetected. "Good, the door's not locked," I breathed to myself. Inside I rummage around the neatly stacked tools, selecting two hammers, an iron chisel and a tommy bar. Quietly closing the door, I make the return trip, still unnoticed, slipping over the wall once more, breathless, but elated. With barely a glance at my new possessions, Jack simply said: "You've been a long time, did Grandad see you?" "Course not, fat-head!"

The old wall was built with mortar and lime, it didn't take long to remove enough bricks to reveal a neat nest built of moss, which sadly was not being used that year! Greatly disappointed, we both agreed it was most unfair of those birds to play a trick on us like that. We were about to replace the bricks we had removed when one of us suggested: "If we took more bricks out, in fact made a hole right through the wall, Grandad, on coming out of his farm-yard could see any traffic coming round the bend sooner." Therefore, we reasoned, it would be much safer for him. Our desire to help Grandad seemed to be overwhelming, and I'm sure not fully appreciated by him!!

Two small boys never worked so hard, once we got a hole right through, leaving the top oval brick capping intact, the hole soon became larger and larger, until it was some six feet long, by two feet in depth. We were covered in brick dust, lime and mortar which stuck to sweat encrusted arms and faces, we stopped for a moment to survey our morning's work.

Suddenly an almighty shout, "What the devil's going on down there?"

Grandad was leaning out of the upstairs bathroom window, his face covered in shaving lather, brandishing his cut-throat razor, he gaped, unbelievingly at the large opening in his brick wall. He must have raced down the stairs two at a time, so quickly did he emerge from the kitchen door. Hurried strides took him across the front garden, soap blowing off his half-shaven face. He confronted us two trembling lads. . . . "We're making a window in the wall, so 'es you can see any traffic coming, Grandad." We replied in unison. Breathing heavily, he grew very red in the face, which even the soap didn't hide. Words failed him. Finally he said: "Come on, into the house, I'll have to see what your parents think of this caper." Giving us both a non-to-gentle shove, he followed behind, muttering away. "Dont know why yer fathers can't teach you two to do something useful for a change. Whatever's my landlord, Toby Sutton going to say. Have to be on to the estate office first thing Monday morning, might even get notice to quit, the least I'll have to do is to pay for the damage."

By now there was an intrigued reception committee at the door wondering what all the sudden commotion was about. Jack and I received a very severe reprimand, even greater than over the cabbage affair, but I must add they didn't beat us, even though we certainly deserved the cane. . . . Perhaps they accepted we had acted in good faith and really were trying to be helpful! We both expressed our deep remorse for a plan that had not met with parental approval.

I understand that Grandfather Perris had a difficult and distasteful

task explaining the damage to estate property. In due course, work-men came to execute repairs, and at Michaelmas there was an addition on the rent for malicious damage.

If one cares to visit Hoe Benham Farm, near Stockcross, in the wall opposite the main farm entrance, can still be seen new brickwork, even though the repair took place over fifty years ago!

Growing Up in the Late '20s and Early 30's

When I look back, the days of my childhood seem to have had a kind of magic about them. They were colourful, exciting, full of discovery, joy, adventurous but yet demanding.

There was a sense of wonderment about our everyday lives – searching for birds nests, tadpoles, frogs and newts. Sliding on a frozen pond on moonlit nights in the crisp, frosty air. I fell very badly on Mr Roy Barlow's frozen pond one cold January evening, but continued sliding across the glassy surface despite loss of blood from badly cut knees!

It was a happy home, close knit with a wonderful father and mother who thought the world of my sister and myself. Late summer brought the smells of homemade jam boiling on an open fire. When winter came, the magic of firelight and stories at bedtime, the closeness of a farming family life. My father's indestructible humour, some of which rubbed off on to us children.

Dymond Farm with its picturesque setting in a dry, low lying valley, with the high ground covered in dense woodlands and the small market town of Newbury just visible through the tree tops to the south. In those days home always seemed to smell of cows – a sweet, grassy, pungent smell, a mixture of milk, warm animals and manure!

There were more farms in our little valley than there are now. Mr Sheppard's swill fed pig farm in Pear Tree Lane, with Messenger Farm at the far end. Wilfred Rowles at Highwood and Red Farm, Mr Lawrence at Grange. The Hosgood brothers and their sister at 'Rookery' farm hand milked a big dairy unit of Shorthorn/Ayrshire crosses. My father's life-long friend, Fred Kimber farmed Cold Ash Farm. Mr Purdue and his son at Fisher's farm.

Most of these have now gone, as single working farm units. Men who didn't work on the farms of the area, puffed into Newbury on their bicycles. There was almost no unemployment.

At school, somebody's Mother was always about to have a baby – we saw birth and death in the farmyard and fields – but we didn't probe, or bother to find out why or where. On one occasion, as twelve and thirteen year olds a gang of us stumbled across a village girl and boy lying close in the thick standing grass. Creeping nearer, heads well down we watched in silence. "I'll bet he's giving her a 'french letter'" one of the older lads whispered knowledgeably.

I remember wondering whatever this youth could be doing with a french letter lying down in a grass field? If he had attended our village school, it was as much as any of us could do to master English let alone read a foreign letter!

Two of us could contain ourselves no longer, we started cat-calling to the courting couple. The young man in the grass half rose and shouted: "Bugger off you lot, or I'll clout yer ears!" We ran off hell for leather, laughing.

Some of the children at our school didn't get enough to eat, no midday meals were available, and it would be doubtful if any food was in the house if they went home in the lunch hour. They were pale and skinny and either died young or grew up weaklings. My sister and I thrived on stews and suet puddings, bread and dripping, jam and fat home cured bacon. Somehow on a great black grate our Mother concocted wonderful meals – tasty and filling. In a great oval pot she cooked hunks of fat bacon from one of our fifteen-score hogs, along with potatoes and cabbage. The vegetables were put into string nets to keep them separate. When they cooked she'd fish them out with the aid of a long fork. Then into the same water she drop a suet roly-poly or a currant 'spotted dick' wrapped and tied at each end in a piece of cloth.

Dad often put down a few wires and came home with a rabbit. In no time at all it would be 'paunched', gutted in other words. Next, off came the skin. Into the oven went the jointed bunny, covered with thickly sliced onions, and halved potatoes smeared with dripping, also a few dumplings to complete the meal. Later we all sat down to a feast fit for a king!

Another big occasion in my youth was pig killing day. Having carefully reared and fattened a docile, friendly baconer for almost a year to a weight of perhaps 300 lbs. it was reluctantly decided – from the pig's point of view – that the day had come. We had need of bacon, hams, belly pork, trotters and all the other nice things that could be made from a well fed carcase.

Father had 'booked' Will Adnams or 'Brusher' as he was known locally to come and do the deed. This nickname had been acquired by the fact that when he wasn't working on the land he spent his time brushing or scrapping off pig hairs!

'Will' lived at No 1 Red Farm Gate. It was always an early start for the gruesome business. My mother rose extra early, preparing dishes and pans, all had their purpose to receive the parts of the pig's anatomy. Dad scrubbed the elm board cutting up table and looked out a nice dry bale of wheat straw.

At 7 a.m. Will Adnams is seen coming up our farm track. He is wearing a brown smock tied around his ample waist with a piece of binder twine. The tools of his trade are wrapped in part of an old sack; humane gun, a sharpening steel, three or four very sharp knives of various lengths and one special knife called the 'pigsticker'.

Dad goes out to the front gate to meet him, myself standing rather nervous in the background. My Mother had already inquired if it was wise for young Bert to witness the slaughter. "Course it's alright boy's got to learn sometime where his grub comes from" Dad replied.

"Mornin' Brusher, picked a nice day for the job, tis a bit too bright to last but twill keep fine 'tut three o'clock when wind and sun gits together then it'll turn wet you'll see, still if all's well we should have our pig killed and cut up by dinner time."

43

We all walk over to a dry clean spot outside of the row of pigsties. "See you got a bale of straw handy Frank, but I reckons we shall need two bales, and a pail or two of clean warm water." A few more preparations, the knives are given a final touch on the steel.

"Let's be having him then" says Brusher. "S'pose you've starved him the last twenty-four hours? Don't want his guts full-o-grub for this job."

Dad now produced a four foot length of stout cord rope with a noose at one end. Entering the pig sty Dad talks quietly "Come on Percy, we got plans for you today." Percy grunts a reply, and comes out of his bedded area. Still talking, Dad rubs its back, now very gently slips the noose of the rope into the pig's mouth, back behind the double row of rear teeth, before pulling the slit-knot tight. Now all hell is let loose, immediately Percy pulls backwards. Once a noose is tight around their upper jaw a pig always goes into reverse, pulling back with all its weight it lets out an ear-piercing, persistent scream. "I've got him," shouts father in triumph.

Brusher rushes in to give a hand on the rope. I give a push on the poor pig's rear. I knew I couldn't get bitten that end!! Percy is dragged and shoved reluctantly from his home and shelter out to the place of slaughter. I suppose my thoughts at that time were a mixture of great interest in the proceedings and yet of horror at what was really a most barbaric act of farm life in the '30s.

Once the poor terror stricken animal was in the chosen spot, Brusher holds the humane gun to its head and pulls the trigger. With a loud crack the bullet is driven into the pig's brain, it immediately slumps to the ground its legs kicking feebly. Now the slaughterman plunges the pigsticking knife into its throat, the main artery is severed. Dad rushes forward with a pail to catch the animal's lifeblood. This, mixed with other ingredients, makes excellent black puddings.

Once the pig is dead, and all movement stopped, the carcase is placed on a pile of clean dry wheat straw, more straw is scattered over it, now its set alight, this will burn off the bristles. Brusher uses a two-grain hay-fork to lightly toss the straw, he wants just enough flame to burn the bristles without scorching the carcase too much, now the pig is rolled over 'to do the other side'. Only the slaughter-man can get the desired result. The blackened carcase is now given a good hard scrub first with warm water now with cold. Any remaining bristles are scraped off. Using a small hook our pig killer deftly removes all eight toe-nails. Two to each foot.

Next the carcase is moved to the barn, a double ended hook is inserted into the sinews of each hind leg at the hock and the whole 300 lbs. of pig meat hoisted up by block and tackle to an overhead beam.

It is truly an hung, drawn and quartered job because now the belly is slit from throat to tail.

My Mother now puts in an appearance, bringing out dishes and a clean bucket for the chitterlings. Onto a large 'turkey' dish goes the heart, liver and kidneys. The pig's head is severed, this will be dealt with later, every little piece of flesh removed and made into brawn.

Taking out the bladder and giving it to me 'Brusher' said "Clean and dry that me lad, it will make you a grand football" and sure enough it was the only one I possessed for many years!

The intestines cleaned with running water, would be used for sausage skins. The backbone was removed, the hams and shoulders dealt with. The two sides of this large pig, after treatment would be our store of winter bacon. They would be placed on a stone slab in the house, to be covered in salt. Turned and re-salted regularly for some three or four weeks until well 'cured'. The hams to be treated in the same way and 'put down' for Christmas. Some pork was cut into small pieces, some to be made into sausages, some to be rendered down into lard, and put into stone jars, later to make delicious pasties and other goodies. Sausages made by my Mother were the real thing – just 'smashing'.

Evening supper on pig killing day was a real treat. Slices of tasty fresh pig's liver fried with onions in a rich brown sauce – delicious. But as we sat round our kitchen table enjoying our meal the sad fact remained that poor ole 'Percy' would not be grunting at the sty door for his breakfast next morning!

Retailing Milk the Hard Way

Early summer of 1933 found us producing far too much milk. Way over what our contract allowed Dad to send off to London each day. Pigs and calves consumed a limited quantity. The rest was allowed to stand overnight in bowls. Next morning my mother skimmed off the cream using her old fashioned brass skimmer. The cream was stored for a week, the first day's skim acting as a 'started', until it was poured into the end over end churn, the wooden lid screwed securely

shut, it was then turned by hand until the butter separated from the butter milk. Kneading out on a clean bench with a pair of butter pats, our special farmhouse butter was made up into decorative one pound packs to be auctioned at Market on Thursday. We also sold cream, and for a time supplied an Italian who made really delicious ice-cream in Bartholomew Street. The problem was , what could be done with the skim milk we had over. Couldn't give more to the pigs. If overfed, they just got fatter and unsaleable.

It occurred to me that maybe our surplus skim milk could be sold to the public. One had to obtain a licence to retail full cream milk, but skim was exempt. I soon found a supply of bottles. Fitting a tradesman's basket on the front of my bike, and a carrier on the back, I set off early one Saturday morning, fully loaded, for the poorer areas of the town. First I tried the Skylings, a tough, rundown council estate, where children ran about barefoot and ragged mites two or three years old stood in gateways wearing just a grubby shapeless dress with no pants on. Why did they always have a snotty nose, dirty faces, and unkempt hair?

The men had left for work, no five day week in those days. I was a slightly built twelve year old and must have looked just a scrap of a lad standing on the doorstep after ringing the door bell holding a couple of bottles of milk. A black terrier flew round the corner of the house to yap in protest. The door opened, a fat lady with a cigarette dangling from her lips and curlers in her hair snapped "Yes, what d'you want?" Holding up my two bottles I said: "Do you want to buy some skim milk, please?" "No, I don't." Bang. The door was slammed in my face. I try next door, ask the same question; the next housewife is a bit more tolerant, and doesn't slam the door. "Skim milk, what's that?" she asked. I explain "The milk that's left after we have taken off the cream." "Can't be no good without the cream. No, I don't want none a' that stuff, thank you very much." I'm getting a bit disheartened, but try again. By now I have half a dozen curious youngsters following me which didn't help at all. Once more I ring a door bell, asking the same question. "Do you want to buy some skim milk?" "No thanks. The milkman's called already this morning." I've always been a persistent character, I press on undeter-red, up one garden path, then another. "Do you want some skim milk, please will you buy some of my milk, only 2½ pence a quart, 1½ pence a pint" I plead. I refuse to give in, it became almost a challenge to sell my first pint. My following of young onlookers had got tired, and given up. There was more exciting things to do on a Saturday than tramping behind this daft boy with his milk bottles! After ringing endless doorbells an elderly lady showed some interest: "Could I have half a pint young man, I live on my own, you see." "I don't sell half pints, Madam." I replied. But not to miss out in making my first sale, I said: "If you have a jug, I'll pour half a pint out of one of these bottles." A quick mental calculation. Half a pint would be three farthings. I couldn't charge that, it would have to be one penny. My spirits rose, I had made a sale.

All that morning I tramped from door to door, council houses, terrace houses, detached residential houses standing well back from the main road with resplendent gardens and well mowed lawns. I was getting very hungry, my stomach told me it was dinner time, I had sold 5 pints. I decided to call it a day. My new venture hadn't been a great success, my takings just seven and half pence.

Next Saturday, undaunted, I tried again. I had learnt a little from last week's experience, had adopted a better sales technique and carefully avoided the doors which had been banged in my face. Slowly, very, very slowly, week by week, my sales began to increase, until I had worked up a round of regulars who liked this pale coloured liquid, also the price was very attractive, being less than half the price of full cream milk. I gave no credit; no cash, no milk, was my motto. Some of the excuses given for not paying there and then were unbelievable. "My husband hasn't given me my housekeeping money yet!" "I've just had to pay the rent, or insurance man." "I've had to buy the children some new shoes" etc. etc. My answer was always the same. "Ok, that's alright, I'll call again next week, you can have some milk then." They soon stopped trying it on!

Doing my milk round early in the morning, I was a bit shocked at first by some of the 'goings on'. Mothers shouted at children, husbands swore at wives. It was not unusual for the door to open and the housewife to be standing there in a most revealing flimsy night-dress. "Oh, the milk boy, come in will you, two pints please, I'll just go and get your money." "Hubby had to go off to work early this morning, would you like a cup of tea?" Each week, my sales increased. I had regular customers with large families.

By now, I was taking a full load, on both front and rear containers of my bike. In fact, I had to start making a return journey for another fill up. I was well pleased with my new business, we were selling all our excess milk production. But, trouble was brewing. One Saturday morning as I rounded the corner into Cromwell Road at Shaw two of the milk roundsmen were waiting for me. "Hi, young 'un. We want a word with you. You're ruining our milk trade. You got no business to be selling that stuff. You gotta have a licence to retail milk." Standing my ground, I replied: "No, I ain't, this is skim milk and not covered by any regulations." "We don't care a bugger what it is. If you are here next week, we shall bash you up, smash all the bottles and throw yer bike in the river." They wandered off, still muttering dire threats. Most distressed, I delivered the remainder of my load. Cycling home, my mind probed for a solution to this threat to my new business venture. I dare not face those two rivals next Saturday, I couldn't ask my father to come round with me, he was far too busy.

Back at home, I unloaded the returned milk bottles and washed them up, put my bike in the shed, then over to the kennel where my faithful old English Sheep Dog, 'Ted' was tied up by a stout collar and chain. When I wasn't at school Ted followed me everywhere, we were inseparable companions, but Saturdays he stayed fastened ouside his kennel. He always looked so disheartened when the milk bike came out. Ted somehow seemed to sense his master had a problem, he rubbed his soft wet nose in my hand and whined as though trying to talk. A vague plan was forming in my mind: "Why not?" I asked myself. "It might work! Ted, how bout you coming with me next week, they dare not come near me with you around." He gave a loud woof, jumped up and almost pushed me over with his great front paws. Next Saturday I got out my bike. Loaded up, Ted knew it was time to be tied up as usual. This time I said, "You're coming with me today, Ted!" He cocked his great shaggy head to one side, with an inquiring expression. He couldn't understand the change in the routine. We set off down the road. It was no trouble for him to keep pace, he had trotted along for miles with me before on other journeys.

We turned left into Cromwell Road, right on time. Sure enough, there they were, waiting for me, as I expected. I stopped at my first customer. They strolled forward menacingly, but I'm sure rather surprised at the presence of my companion. Ted sensed they meant trouble, no one like them would be allowed to approach his master, he gave a deep growl, and bared his teeth. It would take braver men than these to come too close. They kept their distance, undecided what to do next.

At this particular house, there was a large family, and they always purchased two quarts. I marched boldly up the front path, swinging a bottle in each hand. Ted a very obedient dog, was left to guard my loaded bicycle. If need be he would have stayed there for twenty-four hours, and never move. A young lad came to the door with five pennies, the milk was handed over. I walked back down the path. My rivals had left. I never had anymore trouble from them.

1983 and fifty years on. Times have changed. Skim milk now commands a higher price than full cream milk!! I was born too soon!!

1935 – The End of My School Days

With the arrival of the New Year, I was looking forward to the end of my school days. During my first year my attendance had been sporadic. It is two miles each way from our farm to the village school in Love Lane, quite a tramp for a weakly six year old in all weathers, nevertheless I wasn't the only child to undertake such a journey.

In those days, pupils were expected to complete the term following their fourteenth birthday. This meant I would have to stay until the end of the Summer Term, as I would be fourteen years old on May 9th. "Couldn't I leave at Easter?" I pleaded to my parents. "It would be much better for you, Dad, I could help you all through the summer." But my Mother took a firm stand "You've got to stay on until the proper time comes to leave, like everybody else. You should have gone to the Grammar School and got a decent education like we wanted you to, it would always have stood you in good stead. But all you wanted to do was to play around with Albie Raymond and Bertie Goodman, birds nesting and getting into all sorts of trouble. 'Sides, you haven't been at school half the time anyway. Forever getting there late and playing truant." "Couldn't you ask Mr Morris if I can leave Dad" I implored "Perhaps he will be pleased to get rid of me" I added, hopefully.

I quietly slipped out the back door, leaving my parents to continue the argument. The matter was dropped, I had resigned myself to another long term at school, it seemed almost like a prison sentence. I considered running away, but where would I go? If I cycled down to Uncle Sid and Aunt Dorie in Somerset, they'd only send me back, and I'd get a thrashing for nothing. What a silly waste of a good summer, I groaned.

A week went by. It would soon be the Easter Holidays, three weeks off school. I'd have to make the most of the time. Strange how those days flashed by while school days seemed to go on forever.

At breakfast on the last day of term, Dad simply said, "I've made an appointment to see the Headmaster tomorrow." No further explanation was given, but next morning Dad and I set off with Bob pulling the milk float. Bob was Dad's new horse, a chestnut gelding recently bought from Tom Larkcom of Beenham. This cob was a sturdy short-legged animal, not as fast on the road as our previous horse Dick, but useful for some light field-work. We left Bob tied up at the school gate, nibbling tasty shoots of the well-trimmed quick-thorn hedge. Nervously I followed Dad across the playground and round to the Head Master's front door. Two taps on the brass knocker brought light footsteps in the hall, and the door swung open to reveal the neat figure of Mrs Morris. "Mr Houghton, isn't it?" she said, "My husband is expecting you, come in. I will take you through to his Study if you will kindly follow me." Down the carpeted hall, at the far end, she gently tapped on a large mahogany door. "Come in" said a voice. Pushing the door open, she briefly looked inside, and then announced: "Mr Houghton and his son to see you dear."

Mr Morris rose from behind a large paper littered desk, and extended his right hand to Dad. "Good morning sir, take a seat, your son can stand." I stood silent and stiff-legged behind Dad's chair. "Stand closer, boy, it's your future we are here to discuss. Well, Sir, I'm in receipt of your letter, and I note that you wish your son to leave school at the end of this term." He fell silent for what seemed an age, all the time impatiently drumming his fingers on the desk in front of him. Eventually he said: "I've given this case quite a lot of thought. Normally I would turn down your request straight away. Your son has been at this school for, let me see, almost eight years. Regrettably, he hasn't progressed very far academically. His absenteeism being much to blame; lack of concentration on the lesson of the day being another. Therefore I don't consider we can progress much further with his education. I'm sure he will be more useful helping you over the coming summer. Bertie will have to make his living on the land, he has no brains for anything else in life, I'm sorry to say. He can leave my school from yesterday. I will write you a letter of confirmation."

I could hardly believe my ears. My school days were over, one month before my fourteenth birthday. No more sums, learning stupid multiplication tables. English lessons, writing essays on butterflies and things, learning how to spell, what are dictionaries for anyway? ... Trying to sing solo in front of the class as Mr Morris played his violin. With a disgruntled look, he would put his musical

instrument to one side and say: "You and I are in complete dishar-
mony, Bertie, you are singing out of tune, too flat, far too flat, no
tone to your voice at all, and what is more the class cannot hear a
word. Hands up those who could hear Bertie sing? Just two hands
shot up, in the back row, my two pals, supporting me, the rest of the
class sat motionless. Singing lessons were the worst in my mind, to be
avoided at all cost, I would play truant those days, and there was
always the chance that I could persuade Mum to give me a letter
saying I had a headache or something!

Why is it that career selectors consider that if a young country
scholar has no brains, then the only job he or she can do is to work
on the land? Today's farmers and farmworkers need a first-class
education if they are to progress in this very competitive industry.
There is certainly no room for the dim-witted!!

Both men rose from their chairs, Mr Morris came round his desk,
walking over to politely open the door for us. He seemed most
gracious, wishing me well. "And do try and help your parents all you
can, Bertie." he said. "Yes Sir, I'll do my best" I replied, as the door
closed on my scholastic days.

Ploughing and Harrowing

Now that school days were behind me at last, I became a full-time farm boy. Even with my own father as the boss, it didn't make work any easier, and with an early reprieve from any more schooling, I was determined to show my mettle.

When Dad moved to Dymond Farm he sold his Overtime tractor and was once more relying on his Shire horses which my Mother had made him keep. "You'll get tired of that new-fangled tractor afore you're done, you mark my words. Won't start when you want to get on with ploughing, and when it does go, them iron wheels cuts the meadows up dreadfully" she often said.

Boxer and Prince, two dark chestnuts, all of a ton each in weight, were the main task force. They'd work all day at their own steady pace, but had to be well fed. It was amazing how much of our best hay, crushed oats, bran and chaff was scoffed each day. Rose, slightly smaller, a pretty, flea-spotted grey mare, was of doubtful parentage. Dad had picked her up cheap at a farm sale, she had a nasty habit of turning her head round to nip you angrily when one tried to put the collar over her head in the morning. Once harnessed, she was good as gold. Not everyone's ideal horse, too light to go alongside a plough horse, yet too heavy to give any speed in a trap. Rose filled in on odd jobs, muck cart, scuffling, harrowing, rolling or in traces to help the two Shires on extra heavy work.

Dad employed a carter, Jack Little, who lived along the road in a very small cottage with his mother. Berkshire born and bred, his dialect was completely foreign to people from outside the county.

"There's plenty of work for you to get on with" said Dad when the Easter holiday was over. He never allowed field work to be done on public holidays, just milking the cows and feeding livestock. Dad outlined his plans for Spring work on the farm. "I'm going to break up ten acres of old grass this time. Had plenty of muck on it over the years, and pasture's worn out. We'll plant four acres of oats, and six more acres of spring wheat. It's getting a bit late in the season, so we must get stuck into the job, don't want to be sowing cuckoo corn." (The name given to late planted crops.)

At six o'clock in the half-light of morning, Jack was just finishing harnessing up the team. Every horse was groomed with a curry comb, and brushed down before its collar was put on. Jack used to hum as he worked. "Take Boxer to the water trough" said Jack as I arrived still half asleep in the chill of the morning. He had been up feeding his team since before dawn. Boxer farted his way down the steps of the stable and drank his fill of cold water. Then Jack brought down Prince and Rose for their ration.

The field which was to be ploughed was heavy clay, and far from flat. Rose was needed in the traces which meant I would have to lead her. Tandem fashion we made for the 'ten-acres'. Jack walked but he turned to me and said: "Let's give you a leg up, boy-oh, or you'll never last day out!" The heavy single furrow plough was waiting in the next field, where it had recently been used. Mould-board shiny bright with a thin film of cart grease to keep rust at bay. Jack thought the world of his horses and tackle. "Always do a good job for a good master, boy, look after 'un, he'll look after you" was one of his favourite sayings.

Hitching up the horses to the plough, we marked out a land, no sticks or flags; Jack just took a line to some distant tree, unerringly turning over the first spit of green turf, straight as though drawn by an imaginary ruler. Turn on the headland, and back down again, turning out the furrow the other way, thus opening up so that all the land was ploughed. The plough-share penetrated some eight inches into the unyielding clay soil. I walked beside the team as they plodded along, three hundred and twenty yards was the distance from the bottom end to the overground hedge at the top. I often wondered what Jack thought about, as he followed the plough, hob-nailed boots heavy with sticky clay. As we turned on the headland, I had to walk backwards, leading Rose by her bridle at the same time watching my feet carefully, because those big horses had a nasty habit of throwing their feet outwards, and those great steel shoes could almost take your toes off!! You only got them trodden on once – you soon got the message!

Rose had to pull her weight right up to the boundary, and only then with loose traces could she swing round. Jack then tipped his plough onto the bigger of the two wheels, so's it slid along the headland until I turned Rose into the furrow, and once more headed for the other side of the field. Up and down all day. We'd stop for a blow, especially if the horses were sweating.

Twelve o'clock we'd stop for a 'bite o' grub' as Jack called it. I never knew how he told the time, he had no watch, yet he was never more than a few minutes out. He did keep his eye on the sun and if that wasn't shining, there was always the passenger trains that ran punctually through the lower end of the farm. Three-thirty was knock-off time, we had to get back to the stable, unharness, groom, and feed our charges once more. Get them bedded, and settled down for the night. Morning came round soon enough for man, boy and horses.

On a good day we would plough an acre. "If weather 'olds, God willing, we'll finish this bout ole ploughing in nine days, maybe eight if hosses don't get collar sore" Jack announced with confidence. "Rub plenty of alum on those hosses' tender shoulders, it'll harden them, boy."

The next job on our newly ploughed land was to work down a seed bed, before the heavy clay soil baked like lumps of concrete. Jack worked his team with a heavy scuffler or cultivator. I followed with Rose pulling the 'A' harrows. Shaped like the letter, it had a single row of sharp, steel spikes on the outer sides. It gave a fine tilth, and was relatively easy to pull, but it didn't take much of a command from me to cause my horse to stop walking. "Whoa there!" had an immediate effect. In fact as it got later in the day, she would stop for almost any sound, human or animal! "Gee up there, Rose, you knows I never told you to stop!" I give the plough line a sharp swish to slap her flank, then on we'd move again to the boundary ditch, turn and back once more, working down a tilth on a six yard bout each turn.

The seed was drilled with a nine coulter horse drill, no fertiliser. We relied on a good supply of well-rotted dung. I can remember Dad putting on a bit of 'artificial' as he called it, on the mangel-wurzel ground. He would broadcast from a seedlip, superphosphate or potash. The seedlip goes back to biblical times or earlier. A smooth, shallow oblong basket, held from the shoulder with a strong leather strap, it held enough seed grain or 'artificial' to complete one turn.

Dad taught me the art of sowing from a seedlip, but I never managed to get as even a cover as he did. Starting off with your right foot, as it came forward your right hand took a single handful of grain which was scattered in a wide, even sweep before you, covering a five yard wide strip. As your left foot came up, so did your left arm, broadcasting another strip which had to meet up with the first without an overlap. Right, left, right left, – it called for a high degree of concentration. You'd see the results in a few weeks' time, good, bad, or indifferent.

Our seed wheat and oats, planted with the drill, showed through in ten days, straight and true, not even the slightest suggestion of any gap unsown in the whole field. If there had been, Dad would have been the first to chastise Jack. "See, you missed a patch or two up ten acres, carter. Best get up there smartish like, and put things to rights, take a bit of seed and rake it in well, fore neighbours look over fence!"

Camping Days

Just four country lads, all in their early teens, Jack Perris, Dennis Giles, Graham Stanford and myself were to become camping addicts and from that association close and life-long friends.

Jack's father, my Mother's brother, bought his son an ex-army bell tent. The four of us made plans to do some serious camping during the forthcoming summer months. The tent was pitched on a truly marvellous site on Wickham Heath Common. A large natural clearing enclosed and sheltered on three sides by thick gorse bushes yet allowing us a clear view southwards to the high chalk hills of Inkpen Beacon. Moss like grass, soft as the finest Axminster carpet, was kept close cropped by innumerable rabbits.

The tent went up at Easter and we did manage to get a few days under canvas but it was usually during the months from June till September that we seldom missed a week-end.

Once erected our tent stayed up all summer. Our equipment, including a small service tent for storage was quite safe to be left. One could not leave valuable property unattended today. How long before it would be wantonly vandalised, our tents slashed, equipment stolen, perhaps even set on fire? It is a sad reflection on today's society.

Whilst living and sleeping out on the common we were completely independant of our families. It has been asked what four boys did with themselves from Friday afternoon round to Monday morning through the long summer months, but we always seemed to be busy with so many tasks to tackle. I was in charge of the camp fire, collecting and chopping wood to be stored in the dry in our service tent. Dennis was cook, not because he aspired to culinary arts, but simply because he wasn't much good at anything else! We didn't complain, he kept us well fed – albeit mainly from tins. Sausage and beans was Dennis' speciality. Since we didn't possess a frying pan the sausages were carefully wrapped in banana skins to be cooked on the red hot embers, eggs the same way but cracked open into half an orange peel. What a delicious fruity flavour this method produced!

Bacon and fried bread (nearly always burnt black) sizzled in pig's lard on a flat tin tray. If time allowed we made our own bread. First a straight hazel stick was stripped of its bark, next flour and water, mixed together and rolled around the stick to be rotated slowly, baking over hot bricks above the fire. Take out the stick, pour soft butter down the hole, slice and serve with jam, marmalade or honey – delicious!!

Frequent forays were made for supplies, our parents were always quite generous in keeping us supplied with food and there was always our Grandparents just down the hill at Hoe Benham.

After a good meal what nicer way to spend the long cool summer evenings than to sit around the camp fire watching the glow of dying embers with the red glow of the rising moon peering through the tall pine trees, the nightingales start up their evening song, flute-like notes, now a long pause occurs, as though for effect. In the depth of the wood another answers, long-sustained passages of wild melody.

We make plans for the next day before retiring, but not to sleep! Our tent is roomy – some fifteen feet in diameter at ground level, ample room for our four camp beds – yes, we slept in luxury, well up off the cold, hard ground sheet.

Well ahead of our time, we had music. Jack and Graham were the clever pair in electronics. From salvaged bits and pieces they had made a radio, a crystal set, connected to an aerial which wound its way up the tent pole, out at the top and secured to the trunk of a tall pine tree some twenty yards away. Radio Luxembourg came through loud and clear if weather conditions were right, other nights we just couldn't cut out the interference from some rival station. Unfortunately we had only two head sets which meant, of course, that only two of us could listen at once, until such time as our two radio geniuses overcame the problems by fixing up a huge horn speaker!

Another innovation was the fact that we enjoyed electric light, rather weak I must admit, but nothing so primitive as candles for us. Our light was run off an old car battery which had to be frequently charged.

With our radio silent it was pleasant to lay awake and listen to the wild life of the Common. If you kept very, very quiet you could even hear the rabbits munching grass just outside the tent, I wondered if the rabbits had a member on guard because frequently one would give their warning signal. Thump, thump, thump with his hind legs on the ground, perhaps he had seen a fox or a marauding dog. Could even be the local poacher creeping soundlessly to human ears through the pine trees. Armed with a long thin pole, a copper rabbit wire fixed to the top, ready to bring down a roosting cock/pheasant for the pot.

Owls and nightjars called in the night, birds that hunted their prey after dark, the one for voles and mice, the other for insects.

Occasionally, by way of complete contrast to our usual activities all four of us would cycle into Newbury after breakfast on a Saturday morning to catch the 1.30 pm football train to Reading Station. One shilling and one penny each return. In our case not to the match but to watch some live show at the palace theatre!

Apart from a few particularly heavy thunder storms it never seemed to rain, we enjoyed many happy days of innocent, carefree camping, we had no time for girls, no need for money, the only thing which marred those happy days were the 'harvesters' unseen midges which bit us round our tender middles during the night!

War on the Rabbits

I decided to tackle our rabbit problem, not just because they ate or fouled nearly as much grass as the dairy herd, but chiefly because they could be a useful source of income if one could find a market for trapped rabbits, which held a premium over shot ones. In fact some farmers reckoned income from these pests paid the rent.

Having learnt the art and skill of setting snares and traps from my gamekeeper Uncle, I commenced putting this know-how into practice. We had meadows where rabbits had almost taken over. One such meadow at the rear of the piggery had three huge rabbit warrens. The maze of underground tunnels, some going down six or eight feet in the sandy soil with the holes and spoil from below covering a good half acre. Such was the maze of underground passages that ferretting, the traditional method of driving rabbits out to be caught in nets placed over the holes, had limited success. On one occasion we hired the services of a professional rabbit catcher, Micky Warrel from Hampstead Norreys. Full of confidence he arrived early one frosty morning with a dozen trained ferrets, three or four in each little wooden box. Boxes he had made himself, each with a small trapdoor opening on two leather hinges made from discarded horse harness, a flap over a staple held down with a wire nail to prevent the hungry, vicious, cream coloured creatures from escaping. Four of Micky's hunting pack were actually polecats, larger and stronger than the ferrets. They were the 'liners' trained to work down the burrows with a small collar round their necks, to which was attached a strong cord. This played out behind them as they explored below. Providing that they didn't get the cord tangled round a tree root or other obstacle, they could be pulled out again at will.

One of my friends had arrived to help with what we hoped would be an exciting day's rabbiting. From the numbers we had seen nibbling away at our cow pasture at dusk, there must have been at least two hundred white tailed bunnies sleeping down below. Micky gave us a lecture, "When we get out to the first big warren, I'll teach you two how to place the nets. Make sure you push the plug well into the ground, or any caught rabbit will get away." The nets attached to a double cord on two metal rings pulled up tight into a bag, enveloping the unsuspecting rabbit. "You two boys have got to keep quiet, no talking mind, and don't stamp around, the rabbits won't bolt if they knows we're up top waiting for 'em." Working briskly, but quietly in the frosty air, we placed a net over each burrow entrance: "Watch out for pop holes" we were instructed. A small round hole cleverly camouflaged to provide an escape route. These were netted or blocked with earth. Ready at last, Micky proceeded to take some eight or ten of his ferrets from the boxes, holding them gingerly with a gloved hand by the back of their necks, placing each one at a different entrance, watching them promptly vanish below. We all stepped back to await the expected sudden exodus of rabbits. We could hear a lot of thumping and bumping below, but our prey simply retreated into the maze of tunnels. Some two or three hours later, we had lost half our army of ferrets, only two rabbits had been caught in the nets, many had shot out of an undiscovered pop-hole. Lying on the ground we attempted to locate where the ferrets had got rabbits holed up in dead-end tunnels, our ears pressed tight to the

turf to catch any sound of a rumpus below. By pinpointing the spot, we could dig down to retrieve our ferrets and their victims. It was a hit or miss affair, there were no such things like today's radio bleepers which can be attached to a ferret's collar. Scarcely time to eat a sand-coated sandwich, we took turns to dig down following the passage as it dropped further and further downwards. For over an hour we toiled, cursing our uncooperative foes. By the end of a long day we had five dead rabbits for the loss of six good ferrets, a poor exchange rate, the crafty so and so's had beaten us!

This exercise proved to me that you cannot ferret rabbits out of very large deep burrows. Different tactics had to be adopted. The next time I went into town, I bought a large supply of wires and gin traps. Starting round the perimeter of the meadow, I set up my wires in the 'runs' that rabbits make whilst moving to fresh pastures at night. At a spot between one hop and the next, the loop of the copper wire is set at a height of the upright palm of one's hand, held in place by a small hazel twig in which a notch had been cut. The end of the wire is held by a strong piece of cord, which in turn is plugged to the ground by a wooden stake. The rabbit hopping along the same trail nightly cannot see the wire until it is too late; it slips up tight around its neck, and he is throttled to death. A sad but quick end....

Initially, I had great success with my snares, but foxes are the bug-bear, once they got to know an easy supper was being provided they raided my catch every night taking rabbits and wires as well. I did great slaughter with my gin traps, first blocking up any pop-holes, then setting a trap in every burrow entrance, carefully covering the deadly steel teeth with a fine layer of sand, smoothing the surface so that it looked undisturbed. On one end of the trap is a short chain with a ring on the end, through which is passed a stout eighteen inch long wooden peg driven full length into the ground. The rabbit coming out to feed at night, steps on the metal plate, the steel jaws snap shut, and the rabbit is caught usually by one leg. I agree it is a very cruel method to control the rabbits, and I for one am more than pleased that the gin trap is now illegal. The number of times I have almost had my fingers amputated by the careless setting up of a gin-trap should have taught me to have had more mercy for the rabbit.

In general the fox keeps clear of the steel trap, so I slowly gained control of our rabbit infestation, grass began to grow again on pasture where our cows hadn't seen a bite for years.

Soon I was catching so many rabbits that I took to going round my trap line twice a day. Late at night as I tramped across the field, only the sound of my boots on the crisp frost encrusted grass disturbed the silence. Some nights the moon shone so brightly that ghostly shadows were cast on the ground. Moonless nights, the stars shone bright and clear, the Milky Way a broad luminous band of stars, thousands of them giving a surprising amount of light. Then there were the pitch black nights with the wind screaming in fury, driving sheets of icy rain across the open fields. Nearing the burrows, a dull metallic click, followed by a piercing scream. I had driven a rabbit, seeking shelter, onto a trap. With a torch to guide me, I found my traps, removed the victims, and humanely despatched them with a sharp blow with the side of my hand on the back of their necks, killing them instantly. The next step was to hobble them, that is slit one hind leg with a sharp knife, and pass the other leg through, thus enabling them to be carried on a short stick over my shoulder. Then I reset the trap, meticulously removing any sign of the struggle the rabbit had put up trying to escape.

So successful did my trapping become that I had to go round in the mornings with a hand truck in order to bring back my catch. In one season over five hundred rabbits were caught from these three burrows alone!! Alas I discovered that, given three or four weeks' respite, swarms of rabbits from neighbouring areas moved in. So just when I thought I had them beaten, with grass growing green and fresh again, I was back at square one. It was a never-ending battle.

Local butchers purchased a few of the rabbits I caught, perhaps ten or a dozen for the week-end trade, some could be sold in the market auctions, but returns were dismal. Fierce competition was making the sale of my catch difficult. Unsold rabbit carcasses were hung in rows on nails in the back porch, in the wash-house, even in the downstairs loo! – up out of the way of our hungry farm cats. These trapped rabbits were invariably plump, their kidneys almost covered by a layer of white fat, the carcass weighing over 3lbs. After gutting, each providing a solid meal for a family of four for the price of one shilling.

Eventually my Mother began to complain: "It's no good you catching more rabbits until you sell some, if it turns mild they will start to smell." So I went into Newbury on my bicycle, calling at every butcher's shop, but there was just no demand, they all had rows and rows of rabbits in their windows already. "Sorry, me boy,

64

look at that lot, can't sell 'em. I don't want to see another rabbit!" The returns from the rabbit sales were my perks, a way to make a few extra pounds over my wage. I hoped to be able to purchase my own farm one day. It would be a hopelessly slow job if I couldn't even sell my catch! My father came up with a possible solution to the problem. "Get on the telephone to the Rymans in Didcot, they have a large butcher's shop, with wide connections in the meat trade." So I rang up the shop and asked to speak to Mr Ryman senior: "Bert from Dymond Farm speaking" I shouted into the mouthpiece, after all I knew he was over twenty miles away, he wouldn't hear me if I didn't speak up!! "Bert, Bert who?" a deep voice with a country accent replied. "Bert Houghton" I shouted, louder than before. "Oh yes, I've got you now, you're Frank Houghton's son. What can I do for you then? And don't yell down the line so, I'm not deaf!" "I've got a regular supply of good trapped rabbits for sale, can you do with them? I enquired. "Sure, take as many as you've got, ninepence each, send them up by passenger grain to Didcot Station" said the voice at the other end of the line.

I was in business, with an agreed market price. "The money is good, they are sound as a bell" said Dad. Twice a week I took my catch to Hermitage Railway Station. For less than an old penny (240 to the pound) the Great Western Railway transported a rabbit from Hermitage to Didcot! For the next three years thousands made the trip up and over the lonely Berkshire Downs, dumped unceremoniously in the guard's van. Twice a month a cheque came back to me by post. Whilst the money didn't quite buy me a farm, it did eventually more than pay the deposit.

My rabbit catching spread beyond our own farm boundary, I was soon trapping and shooting on neighbours' land. The Second World War had commenced on September 3rd 1939. Overnight the production of our own food became of paramount importance, rabbits and pigeons would have to be kept under strict control, every acre now became vital. An official called to see me, the result being that I was appointed 'part-time Ministry of Agriculture Pest Officer' and for the sum of thirty-five shillings per week, I was expected to control the rabbits and other pests locally. At the same time I was issued with a licence to deal in game.

I restarted my trap line after the War, specialising in catching foxes, badgers, stoats, weasels, moles and of course my old enemy, the rabbit, was still with us. In season I'd skin my catch, nailing the pelts taunt across old doors or wooden planks, rub in salt-petre until the skins were dry and supple. When a suitable parcel could be made up, it would be posted off to Horace Friend Ltd. of Wisbech, skin and feather merchants since 1863.

Price list for 1949, Delivered by post to Wisbech:

Rabbits skins Full grown (winter furred)	4d to 6d each
Hare skins Full grown	9d to 1/- each
Fox skins	2/6 to 4/- each
Badger skins	7/6 to 10/- each
Weasel skins	9d to 1/6 each
Moles (first)	7d each
Moles (seconds)	5d each
Wings and tail feathers: Cock pheasant tail centres	3d each
Cock pheasant tails longsides	1d each
Hen pheasant tails	20/- per lb.

Not until the notorious myxomatosis epidemic in 1954 did we finally have the rabbit population under control.

My First Pig

Thursday is market day in the country town of Newbury. My father was always in attendance, leaving home in the horse and trap as soon as milking and stock feeding chores were completed. He'd come in for breakfast, thick slices of home-cured bacon, fried bread and two eggs, washed down by a large mug of tea. Changing into breeches and gaiters before putting on his highly polished boots. He always left for market smartly dressed. Jack made sure the horse was harnessed and ready between the shafts. Quite often a calf nestled under a net in the milk float on its way to market too. Since leaving school I always made sure I went as well.

I had expressed a wish that I had a pig of my own. A sow, so that I could breed a litter and have some piglets to sell. Dad had business in the dairy section. Looking around the pigs, nearly all pure Berkshires in those days, I noticed a very nice young sow rooting round in her bed of wheat straw. True to her breed, she was completely black except for a dot of white on her rather stumpy nose, four white feet and a patch of white on the end of her curly tail. Approaching the auctioneers clerk I asked for any information about the sow in pen sixteen. "Yes, young man, that sow has been sent in for sale by Miss Rooke of Woolhampton. They are overstocked and cutting back their pig herd. That particular sow has only had one litter. In fact, her six pigs are over there in pen seven – under the wall. They will be sold off separate from their mother." Thanking him, I hurried off to find Dad by the cattle ring. "Dad," I said excitedly, "there's a nice Berkshire sow down the pigs, would you buy it for me?" "No," he replied, "If you wants her, get on and bid for'un. Its your money, you'll be spending, and you got to start sometime, don't go mad though, there's always another day."

Making my way back to the pig section, I was having second thoughts on my plan. Having never purchased anything by auction I began to get cold feet. Little groups of farmers, buyers, as well as sellers, stood around in earnest conversation, snatches of which I overheard, "Pig trade's no good yew, they won't make no money

67

here today, too many people still hay-making after such a wet June, never known it so wet this time of year. Hell of a storm up Lambourn way t'other night, knocked half the corn flat in the valley." "Pigs never were no good in July anyway, no one's going to eat pork if there is no 'r' in the month."

The pig porter, dressed in a brown smock, wheels out a wooden stand, at the back three steps lead up to a small wooden platform, a desk like shelf at the front. This is where the auctioneer will stand to conduct the sale. The porter now goes back to a small shed in one corner of the market, he reappears enthusiastically ringing a large hand bell. It is twelve noon the sale of the pigs is imminent. A few minutes later Mr Watson makes his way towards us followed by a young clerk carrying the list of vendors with their lot numbers. Apparently Mr Arthur T. Watson has been selling the pigs for many years. A big man with a very red face, he sports a large walrus moustache. On his head a wide brimmed trilby hat. Summer and winter, rain or shine he wore a mackintosh reaching almost down to his ankles. He mounts the three steps on the sale platform, indicates to the bell ringer to stop. "Come on then you eager buyers, bid up and we'll soon get this job done." The porter climbs over the iron rails into the first pen of pigs. Holding one of the litter aloft for all to see. The bidding commences. A rough looking character taps the pigs on offer with a hazel thumb stick. He wears a cloth cap at a rakish angle. His ragged tweed jacket, which obviously has given long service, is stiff with dried pig meal.

"Fifteen bob, Sir," he shouts out. The bidding rises in sixpenny bids until the hammer falls at eighteen shillings and sixpence. Buzz Dewe's, the buyer. "Next lot", says Mr Watson. The clerk writes down the purchaser and the price. Quickly each lot is sold. The wheeled stand is moved up the line of pens. All the pens of weaners under the wall are quickly sold, we all move across and selling starts down the next row. Reaching pen sixteen 'my' sow was about to be offered for sale. In my mind's eye she was already mine! Mr Watson gave a brief summary. "This young Berkshire gilt, pure bred she is, but no pedigree with her, comes from Miss Rooke's well known herd at Woolhampton, only selling because they're overstocked. I have just sold her first litter of six pigs, made a guinea each, top price today." "Now, this pig has got all her life in front of her, what am I bid?" "Who'll put her in at eight pounds, seven? well, six, surely?" He looks round the silent crowd. I raise my right hand slightly.

"Three pounds, Sir!" "Well!! I don't know," says the auctioneer, "one bidder is worth a dozen onlookers I suppose?" "Three pounds, I'm bid, three pounds, three pounds." He takes another bid, someone nodded on the far side of the crowd. "Three pounds five shillings" I lift my hand a few inches, forefinger extended. "Three pound, ten shillings, three pounds fifteen shillings." The same man bids again. This time I look up at the auctioneer, give a quick wink of one eye. "Four pounds, the starters in, any advance?" The hammer's poised, about to fall. "Half-a-crown," says my opponent in a loud voice. Again I bid, this time the hammer bangs on the little shelf. "Four pounds, five shillings." Mr Watson looks quizzically down at me, "Name, young man?" "Bert Houghton" I replied. I had just bought my first pig.

As the years passed by I was to purchase many hundreds of stock in Newbury Market before it finally closed in 1969, and never once did I need to announce my name again!

I hurried up to the cattle ring to tell Dad the good news. "I've bought that gilt, Dad." "Oh, well done, better go over to Dreweatts' office and pay if you've got enough money on you" was all he said.

After the market sale was over we went into the Victory Cafe to get a late lunch. The same little circle of Dad's business associates tagged along too. Seriously discussing prices of the day, deals struck, profits made. By the end of the meal and after a few drinks, things had livened up somewhat. Loud laughter followed coarse jokes, dubious stories were told. We had a room to ourselves in the cafe, eight or ten sitting round one long table. Finally the meal ended: "Who's turn to pay this week then?" says Jeff Ryman sitting at the top end of the table: "I paid for all, on'ee last week, in case you have all forgotten." "When did you pay last, Tom," says someone else looking across at a fat red faced farmer, keeping very quiet. My father cuts in, "Fairest way is to toss for it, get your coins out, odd man out, goes out." Round the table hands delve into trouser pockets, large, work hardened hands slap a coin on the table. By a series of eliminations we get down to the last two. Jeff Ryman is one of them. "This is a set-up, you chaps are working it somehow, I paid last week, remember?" "Come on, toss the bloody thing then" he says crossly. Up goes the coin, he calls: "Heads it is" as it bangs down on the table. The other man's hand lifts slowly off the table cloth. Jeff glances at the silver shilling. "Bugger, I've lost again!" he roars good humouredly. "Now you all had enough to eat and drink, cos I'm paying?" Someone slaps him on the back, "Better luck next time Jeff!" "Who says there's going to be a next time?" he replies. With that we all rise and reaching for hats, coats and walking sticks we go back to the market to load our stock.

Back to the now half-empty livestock market, most of the stock had been loaded or walked to the railway station on their way to new destinations or a slaughter house. Our horse Beauty, still harnessed and between the milk float shafts had been tethered to a rail at the back of the market. Earlier Dad had slipped the nosebag over her head which contained a small amount of bait as he called it. "Hoss as got to eat same 'as us," he would say. We now reversed the cart to a raised loading bay, showing my payment pass to the porter, we were allowed to load my sow. A pig net tied down tightly prevented any escape. I had to sit on a cushion at the rear otherwise with Dad sitting up front to drive, there would be too much weight on the horse's back. Swinging out into Market Street, then right down Bartholomew Street over the water bridge, into Northbrook Street. Beauty knowing she was homeward bound kept up a fast trot. By the mid thirties there was quite a lot of motorised traffic in the town, a few farmers were still using horse drawn vehicles. Phil Froude of

Bucklebury Slade regularly came to market with a horse and trap every Thursday well into the 1960s.

Back home again my sow was off-loaded into one of a row of pig-sties which Dad had built close to the cowshed some years previously. These buildings, long since demolished stood close to the little bungalow called 'Briarlea'.

The milk float was reversed into a shed, tipped up to keep the shafts off the wet ground. Beauty unharnessed and released, kicked up her heels, toss her head and gallop out into the green meadow in sheet delight, her day's work done. She'd roll on the grass on her back, all four legs flaying, but never quite roll right over. Scrambling to her feet she'd now have a good shake before, head down, to eat her fill of grass.

In great excitement I ran to the farmhouse: "Mum, Delcie, come and see my sow, I bought it at the market!" We hurry back across the paddock to the sties. Mum agreed it was a nice young sow. "Well, I hope you keep her fed and cleaned out, no good getting tired of the job after a few weeks, and expect your father to do it, he's got more than enough to do." "What do you plan to do with her, now you've got her?" "Breed some pigs, Mum, let her have a litter, then sell them when they're eight weeks old and make a profit, might keep a couple of gilts out of the litter, Dad says I can fatten a lot of pigs later on, he might put me up a piggery!" "H'm, well its good you've got ambition, I'm sure Dad will help you to get a start, but you'll have to work hard. Now go and give your father a hand with the milking whilst I get supper ready." I ran off to fetch the dairy herd in. That afternoon I milked cows with a renewed enthusiasm.

Three days later, my sow didn't eat her food, she rooted restlessly round the sty, then with front feet over the gate she seemed to want to get out. "She's coming into season" my father explained. "Mr Purdue at Fisher's Farm as got a Berkshire boar, give her another couple of days then we'll walk her over there." Two mornings later, Dad said, "We'll take your sow to the boar today. Don't feed her this morning." Milking done, we had a quick breakfast then I went down to the sties and opened the gate, out she came with a rush and for a few minutes snorted and barked as she gambolled around the paddock. Up to now she had just been 'my sow'. Mum said to me: "You must give your pig a name, call her Bessie", so Bessie she became.

Dad and I guided her across the fields, tapping her sides with a flat stick. Into Well Meadow behind Easton Copse we crossed the little brick bridge, then on across the meadows of Fishers Farm, our journey took only about twenty minutes to reach the farm buildings. Mr Purdue, noticed our approach, rattled a galvanised bucket, we did the last hundred yards at a trot!! At the rear of the barn, a row of traditional brick built sties held half a dozen sows and litters and a very large rather ancient looking Berkshire boar. His tusks looked deadly, curving out and upwards from his lower jaw. On opening the sty gate, Bessie was quick to enter but at first showed animosity to her intended lover. Charlie, as the boar was called, soon got amorous in a rather brutal way. Champing his great jaws, frothing at the mouth, he hooked Bessie under the belly with his snout, lifting her back legs right off the ground. This foreplay didn't last long, Bess stood rigid as he mounted her.

Dad kept a bull, and I had seen him perform on many occasions, a bovine mating was just a quick jump and it was over, but with these two pigs coupling went on and on for ages.

All the while Dad and Mr Purdue leaned on the sty wall, deep in conversation. "Putting the world to rights" they called it. Finally, exhausted, Charlie slid off his mate. "That's about it, young man, your sow should be alright now for a dozen pigs," said Mr Purdue. Turning to Dad, he said "'Bout coming in the house for a cup of tea, give them two pigs time for another go, just to make sure, like."

Dad and I follow as he led the way across the yard. Into the four hundred year old brick and timbered farmhouse. Dad, a tall man ducks his head as he enters. Massive black oak beams support the rooms above. Lattice, leaded windows let in little of the bright July sunshine. Their collie dog lies curled up asleep on the settee. Tea is soon brewed: "What about you Bert, rather have lemonade this hot weather?" "Yes, I would, thank you." I replied. "'Bout a slice oh mother's 'pudden' cake to go wheat?" was his next question. Mrs Purdue emerges from the kitchen with the welcomed refreshments. Turning to me she enquires: "Are you pleased you've left school then?" What a daft question, silly woman, the thoughts cross my mind. "Yes," I reply, "I never liked school much."

The lemonade is refreshing, the 'pudden' cake goes down well. The two men are still discussing the ups and downs of farming. Time to be leaving. Mr Purdue looks at me and says, "This boar job, cost you a quid young man, course you can bring her back if her returns to service." "I've brought some money." I reply, taking a pound note out of my wallet. "Good, going to be like yer Dad, aye? pay on the nail?" "What I likes to see that is, you'll get on in this world if eh does that. Ben't no good owing money to people, nor borrowing it. I've never borrowed a penny in me life, and I'm telling ya I bent going to start that caper now." Good sound advice, but I'm afraid I haven't always followed it.

Ten weeks pass by. I noticed that Bessie came out of her pen much slower for breakfast these days, and her belly was definitely swelling. At twelve weeks, Dad looked over the sty one morning when I was cleaning out, casting an eye over my sow he said: "She looks promising." By now her pendulous udder almost touched the ground. A sow is pregnant sixteen weeks. "When her time is up, draw a teat whilst she's feeding, if you gets a spot of milk, she'll pig within twenty-four hours." Dad explained.

November was almost out, one morning Bessie was giving motherly grunts and waddling heavily round her sty with a mouthful of straw. I knew she was making a nest for her piglets. I didn't have to draw her teats, little drops of milk were already dropping from each one. All that day I found jobs close by but there were no further developments. I stayed with her until midnight, but she had settled down, it seemed for the night.

"Com'on to bed, she'll manage without your help," said my mother. I hurried down early the next morning, I knew something had happened before looking in the pen, I could hear Bessie grunting happily and lots of high pitched squeaks. It was a dull wet morning, inside the farrowing pen the light was poor, but I could see my sow lying on her side and a whole row of tiny Berkshire piglets having their first suckle. I counted ten little backsides, tails wagging merrily. They stopped sucking as quickly as they started, new born pigs take milk little and often. Then as is their custom, one of the piglets went up to the mother's snout to say: "Thank you" I never did discover if it is always the same one!!

I ran back to the house in great excitement to break the good news to my parents. "Come and see them, you too Delcie, they're lovely!!"

The date recorded in my diary at the time was 29th November 1935.

One hundred weight (112 lbs.) of meal cost seven shillings and ninepence, skim milk, purchased from my father cost four old pence for two gallons. I bought a brass ring to put in Bessie's nose at one shilling and two pence. An expensive luxury, but a necessity to prevent her grubbing up the pasture when I let her out to roam with her litter. One piglet died, it was always the weakling, a 'darling' Dad called it. I sold my litter of pigs when they were nine weeks old, on January 30th 1936. They made exactly one pound each in Newbury Market. After commission and tolls my cheque was £8-9-0. Bessie reared six more litters before she herself ended up as sausages.

I Purchase a 'Bobby' Calf

Between the daily chore of milking our small dairy herd, I accompany my father on his visits to other farms in the district, buying and selling livestock. The harvest was in full swing, Dad was busy too, when one morning, September 11th 1935 to be exact, he said to me: "Old Froudie", meaning Mr Froude of Manor Farm, Oare (a small hamlet just north of Hermitage) 'as got a bull calf to sell. Get on yer bike, and buy it off him, but watch it, he's a sharp old customer, he'll sting you with the price given half a chance." "Here, take a bit of cash, that will tempt him."

Out comes my cycle, in no time at all I cover the four miles, turning into the farm yard just as Mr Froude comes out from breakfast, no doubt having consumed a large plateful of rashers and eggs. He recognised me and looking rather surprised said, "Come on yer own today then, where's the old man, he ain't going to trust you to spend his money, is he?" "Dad's busy" I replied. "Oh, ah, got up late morn'n likely," was his answer. "Well come and have a look at a nice bull calf, hope he's sent some money, I can do with it?" Walking up through the yard, I felt very important, but also rather nervous. I was determined to be careful parting with my money. We stop at the door of a loose box. "in 'ere" said Mr Froude. Inside a pathetic little Guernsey calf lies in one corner. Our farmer lifts the little animal to its feet: "What are you going to give me for him then?" I was asked. "Well really, Mr Froude, he's hardly worth the transport to fetch him, but I'll give you ten shillings for him." "Don't insult me with a price like that young man, calf's wo'th thirty-shillings if he wo'th a penny." I knew his asking price was far too high, I would have to tread cautiously. "No, I'll make it twelve shillings." I replied. "Give us a quid for him, can't waste all day selling a calf I got work to do." "Fourteen shillings, can't give a penny more" says I. "You're worse than your father, and he's bad enough. Alright young man, you can have 'im, don't say I never helped you in life!" "Give us your money, better fetch the little bugger by tomorrow, he's drinking nye on a gallon of milk a day."

On market day, Dad had a few more calves to collect around the district with the horse and milk float. My first 'bargain' was picked up with the others which were mainly shorthorn or shorthorn crosses. Protesting loudly under the mesh of a rope net, they didn't seem to appreciate a pleasant canter through the picturesque Berkshire countryside. Over the bridge which spans the River Lambourn at Shaw. At the south end of Shaw Crescent just a tee junction where the Hermitage road joined the A4. No Robin Hood Roundabout for our horse-drawn transport to negotiate, thank goodness! Turn right into town, Beauty trots smartly up Northbrook Street, joining other market day transport as we turn into Market Street.

Our horse slows to a walk as we join the throng with our load of calves, it means queuing for a while before we get to the Sale Ring, where they are to be off loaded. One by one the auctioneers' porter lifts each reluctant calf from the rear of the carts. Dragged along by a rope round their necks, they dig their feet into the concrete refusing to move their legs. The bad-tempered drover lifts the poor calf's backside off the ground by means of a tug on its tail. "Come on you little bugger, move yer self."

Dad turns to me and said, "Leave your calf in the float, you can try and sell it privately, that way you will save on the auctioneers commission. Stay there, I'll send Mr Herbert Holdstock round, he'll buy it off you, he has those bobby calves killed at Reading Abattoir for veal and ham pies. A few minutes later, Mr Holdstock came across to me, he was smartly dressed in a Tweed check jacket, collar and tie, trilby hat, corduroy breeches and a pair of highly polished boots and gaiters. The traditional dress for a prosperous country gentleman of that period. Little time was wasted in the transaction. My asking price was twenty-five shillings, and was more than pleased to accept twenty-one shillings. It is recorded in my diary that I paid Dad sixpence for transport, leaving me a profit of six shillings and sixpence on my first deal, 33%.

Note: The expression or name 'bobby' calf applies to a very young calf that has no future for breeding purposes or as a beef animal, and is expected to be slaughtered at a few days old.

Pig Farming

1937 – sixteen years old, having already worked full-time at Dymond Farm for over two years, for just a small wage, plus any extras I might be fortunate enough to earn on the side. Dad did business with the Taylors of Oare. He came home quite excited one afternoon, "The Taylors have gone into pigs in a big way," he informed my Mother and I. "They have erected two Danish type piggeries, the most modern in the country. The inside air temperature is controlled. The pigs are in pens with a dung passage at the rear where they do all their business. Shut the pigs in the sleeping quarters and you have a clear passage to muck out everyday. And you will not believe this," he continued even more excitedly, "there is a central feed passage for the pigman to push a feed truck down, measuring out a given amount of balanced meal with a scoop according to the size and number of pigs in each pen. Then he returns to the meal house, takes a second truck, this time with water, pours a set quantity onto the meal in the glazed earthenware trough and the pigs mix their feed themselves!" This fast ingenious way to feed pigs was what Dad couldn't get over. "Why hadn't anyone thought of such a simple solution before? It seems like they have been using this method in Denmark for some time, no wonder the Danes turn out cheaper bacon than we do!"

Today wet feeding of meal and water would seem very old fashioned, but you must remember that previously small farmers like ourselves had mixed barley meal, sharps or middlings with a small amount of fish meal in a used beer barrel butt. Simply pour in enough water to make a sloppy mix, stirring these very basic ingredients with a stout hazel stick or a small shovel. This was fine until a prolonged frost set in, the mixture then froze during the night round the inside of the barrel, with each frosty day the unfrozen centre got smaller and smaller. The pig conversion rate was disastrous on such ice-cube rations. To carry bucket after bucket full, hands cold and wet, pour into the pig trough with a dozen porkers all trying to get their heads in the bucket at once, was cold work. We wore an old West of

England sack as an apron at feeding time, but it didn't help much – we still got saturated. I've known the time on those very frosty mornings when if you didn't wear gloves your hands froze to the metal bucket handle. Dad took me to see those luxurious pig palaces at Oare. The largest piggery held three hundred and sixty pigs, the other just one hundred, staggering numbers, this was factory farming although I didn't realise at the time. Anyway the expression hadn't yet been coined.

"Would you like a nice new piggery like that, start pig farming on your own account? Dad inquired of me? "You mean, you would get one built, like that, just for me, Dad?". "Sure I will" he replied. "Best way to learn a business is to set up on your own, use your own money win or lose, people keep a tight hold on the reins if its your pound notes at stake." If I get the piggery built on my land, you can then pay me a small rent, buy your own pigs and food out of your savings, invest some of that rabbit money you've got stacked away."

In the Spring of 1938, my Danish piggery was erected, purchased from Pratten & Co. of Midsommer Norton, in Somerset. It cost a total of £342:-

Piggery for one hundred fat pigs:

Delivered and erected for a total sum of	£342-0-0
1 Wheelbarrow	£1-6-0
One ton of straw	£1-0-0
Two feed trucks £5 each	£10-0-0
Tar to preserve outside woodwork	6-6
Gallon container of worm powder	11-0
Weigh Crate	£14-5-0

The piggery was built completely in seasoned timber with an asbestos roof. Two skilled workmen came up from Somerset a few days in advance. They marked out the site, dug foundations, and laid a concrete base on a brick surround. Next came the house itself, the whole lot on one lorry, with sections already made, the bottom half of each section double lined for insulation. The work was completed in one week, by just those two men. £342 seems an unbelievably small sum to pay for a piggery with a capacity to fatten a hundred bacon pigs, with a large feed store on one end, until one remembers that Dad's modern farmhouse only cost £750 to build six years earlier.

Over the years I kept my pig house in good repair. Black creosote was applied to the pens to prevent the pigs chewing the woodwork, the windows and gutterings painted white, whilst the outside had a coat of tar annually. This thick, black liquid was purchased from Newbury Gas Works, five gallons for one shilling. if the weather was cold, I would heat up this smelly substance over a small fire, great care being taken not to bring it to the boil, otherwise it boiled over, and the whole lot went up in flames.

It speaks well of the material used and the craftsmen of the day, that our piggery is still in good shape after fifty years of continuous production. I cannot remember there not being some pigs in occupation even during some of the worse 'downs' in the pig price cycle.

The building was severely damaged by blast from a doodle bug which fell on Shaw Farm in 1944.

Inside the piggery, there were ten individual pens, each holding ten piglets, with trough room up to bacon size. My aim was to purchase eight week old weaner pigs at the rate of ten every fortnight. Thus the house would be full after twenty weeks, just about the time that the first bacon pigs would be going off to market at two hundred pounds live weight, to kill out at one hundred and fifty pounds or seven and a half score (score being twenty pounds). Once the piggery was full, this method would give continuous production, turning out lean bacon on a conveyor system. Farmers came from all round the district to see our Danish Piggery.

My farm diary of 1938 confirms that the first nine store pigs took pride of place in the new piggery on April 27th. Purchased from a Mr Ralph of Hampstead Norreys for twenty-two shillings each a total of £9-18-0. I paid a haulier five shillings to transport them by horse and trap. Half a ton of pig food (meal) cost four pounds, twelve shillings and sixpence. Eleven days later, on May 7 1938 I invested twenty-two pounds, ten shillings on twenty store pigs purchased from my grandfather. I was filling the piggery faster than anticipated, because on May 31st twenty-two more pigs were purchased from a Mr Bounds at twenty-four shillings each. Either pig prices were on the rise, or word had got around that I was a keen buyer and anxious to fill my new piggery, because I see that by June 8 I paid a Mr Skuse of Upper Basildon twenty-five shillings each for twenty-two pigs, a total of almost twenty-eight pounds, but I beat the carrier down in price, it must have been at least twelve miles each way, I only paid him two shillings and sixpence (12p) to bring them over!

My first sale of fat hogs was made on 29th August 1938, to Mr

Wilfred Rowles for £4-15-0 each. Twenty more on October 11th for a total of £103-9-7. That is, just over £5-0-0 each. The piggery has a low ceiling with a layer of straw above which keeps the air temperature cool in Summer, and warm in Winter, therefore the pig conversion rate is very good. On average the pigs fattened on four pounds of balanced ration per day, twenty-eight pounds weight in one week, or put another way, approximately one hundred weight per month. At nine shillings per cwt. it cost 45/- to keep a pig for five months! When they went out fat, they cost me about four pounds each allowing a little for rent of house, water and straw. My profit was £1 per pig, a return of 20% on capital. Few pig farmers can achieve that level of profitability today.

By November, the piggery was full, I now purchased from Messrs. Silcocks & Co. two tons of 'Danex'. This was a large order to deliver to one farm and I had a special price of £17-7-0. One month later on December 12th, the price had fallen to £7-7-6 per ton. The next step was to obtain a market for quality bacon pigs. A contract was negotiated with Bowyers of Trowbridge for an agreed number per month. These pigs had to kill out at a carcase weight of 140–150 lbs (i.e. 7 to 7½ score), lean, and with an overall length of so many millimetres. The price was 13/6 per score, £5-0-3 for a 7 score baconer. Not a high price, but the main advantage was that this price held for one year, and one could plan ahead.

By 1941, store pigs had arisen in price to around two pounds each. Pig meal was now twelve pounds per ton, and it was on ration. We had coupons to allow us as farmers to purchase a given quantity for the month. Our hogs had to be transported to Newbury Market, and sold at the ruling government imposed price – for example, on 25th August 1941, four fat hogs made £29-14-0, not each one! That was the total return.

After the war, in the early 1950's, store pigs eight weeks old had a value of £5 to £6 each. Fat hogs made £17 to £20 each. At the time of writing this section in January 1987, todays 25–30 kilo live weight weaner commands a price of £25 to £30 each. A balanced ration in nuts or pellet form, costs £180 to £200 per ton, and the finished bacon pig (not fat hogs anymore) £70 to £75. These pigs bear little resemblance to the fat, short, chunky Saddleback Cross Large White (blue and white) which were the original occupants of my Danish Piggery.

My First Gun

"How about buying me a gun, Dad? Help to keep the rabbit numbers down, I could have a go at all the rats around the buildings, shoot some of the other vermin too." "You will have to wait until you're older, sixteen is too young to walk around with a loaded shotgun" replied my father.

We were now living in the new farmhouse, my Mother hadn't really liked 'Briarlea', the little two-bedroomed bungalow. Dymond Farm house was built on an open field site. Compared to the bungalow it was a spacious and even luxurious dwelling. My parents had accepted the lowest tender from a local building firm. Unfortunately with the construction of the building only half-completed, the firm went into liquidation. Mr Faithful of Shaw took over the uncompleted work. The bungalow had been let to tenants. Dad was responsible for outside maintenance, and a good coat of paint was badly needed.

Dad relented over my request for a gun and suggested a solution. "Clean the old paintwork down, putty in where needed round the glass, give all the woodwork three coats of paint, and I'll buy you a gun." Dad announced one day. I was quick to say 'yes' to that offer, it was summer time, with long day-light hours, and we were not too busy on the farm. Working only in my spare time, the job was finished in five weeks, and in my opinion it looked really smart, the place was transformed, it had looked quite tatty before!

Dad kept his word and purchased a new single barrelled four-ten, plus a box of 50 long shot cartridges. It came from Thomas Turner of Northbrook Street, Newbury, and cost thirty-seven shillings and sixpence, two pounds with the cartridges. I was soon bowling rabbits over like ninepins. My gun had a killing range of fifteen yards, even twenty on occasion. Early morning or at dusk, I'd creep up on them Red Indian style. I had great sport on winter days; place a ferret into a shallow burrow, stand back, and keep very quiet, and the rabbits would come hopping out, a simple target especially if the ground was snow covered. Carefully concealing myself in well made hides, the wily woodies crashed to the woodland carpet as they glided into roost at dusk.

It was not until after the War that I purchased my next gun, a double barrelled twelve-bore hammer gun of unknown origin. Very second-hand, I bought it from my game-keeper uncle for ten pounds. Thousands of cartridges were fired from this old musket which now resides in 'retirement' above the mantelpiece in my farmhouse lounge. As it gathers dust, I often think of those days when a particular high curling pheasant dropped out of the sky from a well-aimed shot.

Growing Up

Prior to joining the Armed Forces, I was helping my parents with daily chores on their small holding. Our immediate neighbour, Eli Cross, was the tenant farmer of Mousefield Farm. He milked a small herd of commercial Guernsey cows, retailing the high quality milk in the Newbury area, under the name of Mousefield Dairy Products.

The Cross family were very hardworking; Mr and Mrs Cross had just one son, Norman (now farming near Bacup, in Lancashire) and four attractive daughters. My sister Delcie and I had been to the occasional Birthday or Christmas Party at the farmhouse, but now I found myself taking more than a passing interest in Patricia. Well aware of the fact that, although only sixteen, she had very blue eyes, a pleasant smile, and lovely long blonde hair! My father was not pleased by the fact that I was giving Mr Cross a helping hand on more than one occasion, especially if it meant working alongside Pat.

Haymaking time, whilst hard work, brought all the family out into the field. We seemed to get glorious, long hot summers. Those were the days of ricks. The hay when mellowed and wind-dried was raked up into windrows with a horse drawn rake. Eli farmed with the aid of two magnificent Shire horses. Those two pulled a large wooden tined hay sweep, one horse on either side with Pat's father sat on the iron seat at the rear in full control. "Gid up thir" he would say, in his guttural voice. Swinging out across the meadow to sweep in yet another great stack of hay, half a wagon load at one hit. Coming back to the elevator one horse on either side of the windrow they'd throw their great weight into their collars, putting all their strength against the traces. The elevator was driven by an old horse going round and round in a tight circle, carefully stepping over the drive shaft every time around. Frequently old Ned would came to a stop for no reason at all, but a loud curse from the rick-builder made him reluctantly plod on.

My job was to help Pat fork the hay into the elevator, now if one could keep each load clear, it was not too bad, but if you got behind and another sweep load was jammed on top of the first, it was the devil's own job to untangle. We longed to see the sweep set off for the far side of the meadow. Redouble our efforts, we may get time for a cool drink and a few minutes sit down in the shade of the rick. We even prayed for a heavy shower, then work would stop for the day!!!

I didn't seem to feel muscle aches or blistered hands if it served as an excuse to share Pat's company, and there was always romantic walks in the woods later in the day as compensation. I should add that our courtship never progressed beyond the kiss and cuddle stage, even so, we had great fun for a few short years. It wasn't all work at Mousefield Farm, we did get some leisure time.

Mr Cross drove a large buff coloured two seater Buick, under a long bonnet was a massive V8 engine capable of driving this monster of a car at one hundred miles per hour. This vehicle was Pat's father's pride and joy, and he kept the chrome and brasswork immaculate. Two great brass headlamps lit up the road at night. The seats upholstered in real leather were rather a sit-up-straight affair, but one got a good view of the surrounding countryside on a journey. We seldom missed an Agricultural Show, cross-country event or point to point. Mr Cross, smartly dressed in breeches and gaiters, his wife always well dressed for the occasion too, both sat up front. Pat and myself clambered into the rear dicky seat. It could be cold in the back at seventy or eighty miles an hour, but it was a good excuse to snuggle up close under a heavy car rug and let the scenery flash past. It was a fast car for those days, it's driver claimed that it was so heavy, and held the road so well, he could leave go of the steering wheel on straight stretches and write a letter!!! If he was catching up with the farm correspondence, we ignored the fact, sitting in the rear!

I enjoyed the dark, cold winter evenings during this happy period of my life, spending more and more time at Mousefield Farm, sitting with this jovial farming family in front of a huge log fire, even though it meant listening to Mr Cross repeating once more his far-fetched stories. Old fencing stakes, even half a tree, reached out from the fire halfway across the room, he never seemed to saw his firewood to a sensible length. "Push those logs in Bert, she's starting to smoke again" he would order. No such thing as television, of course, not even a radio, we made our own entertainment, playing cards, chess, dominoes, postman's knock at Christmas time!! Other members of the Cross family never ceased to tease me, because I was always combing and brushing Patricia's long blonde hair, but we were sixteen years old, she was my girl, we had ambitions for the future, we would have our own farm in due course.

All those day-dreams were to be shattered a year or two later by a certain upstart named Adolf Hitler. Both Pat and I were eventually to join the Royal Air Force, myself as a trainee pilot, she as a heavy truck driver.

When we did meet again after the War, she was married with a young family, and I was courting a land army girl called Peggy Day! They say the wheels of fate rotate in mysterious ways!!

Teddy

1939. There was much talk of war with Hitler. England imported a large proportion of its food supplies. Home production would be vital if we were to avoid starvation. Old pastures must be ploughed, more cereals grown. "We should buy a tractor" I suggested to my father. "No good relying on horses if we have to plough up more land."

We couldn't afford a new one, and second-hand tractors were scarce. The next time Dad and I had cause to visit Reading livestock market, we called on Walter Wilders, as luck would have it, they had an excellent second-hand standard Fordson on their books. This 1934 model had been well maintained, so they said, and had only had one owner.

It was the water cleaner type, ran on T.V.O. (Tractor Vaporising Oil), and mounted on iron wheels with spade lugs for traction. The price was £120, cash. If we didn't want it they had a dozen other farmers desperate for a good tractor.

"You will want a plough as well, Mr Houghton, can't hitch your horse plough behind this chap, you know. She'll pull two furrows anywhere, sand or clay, up hill or down. I got just the job. Two furrow international semi-digger, new turn furrows and land-sides, £80. £200 will set you and your son here up proper. You will soon get on top of your work, get your lad to contract jobs for your neighbours, going to be plenty of call for a good tractor if them damn Germans play rough again."

On the way home, Dad said: "You better tell your mother we have bought a tractor and plough, she won't be very pleased, us spending so much money." I broke the news gently. Surprisingly, she wasn't too cross. "If we get a war we will need a tractor, that's if you can get fuel for it?" Of course, Dad and I hadn't thought of that, it wouldn't run on crushed oats!!

The new tractor was to be called 'Teddy', after my faithful old English Sheepdog who had met an early death through eating poison bait.

It arrived a few days later, both tractor and plough on a low-loader, a great day for me, as few of our neighbours owned a tractor at the time. Grease and dust accumulated over previous years had been removed, the paintwork touched up, the many grease nipples showed evidence of the grease-gun. The single word 'Fordson' in raised black letters on a white background showed proudly on the front of the radiator for all to see.

'Teddy' had a shed all to himself. I had spent some days getting everything ready for his arrival; wheel jack, hammer, plug spanner, oil can, grease gun, funnel and other bits and pieces I had thought necessary for his maintenance. Two hundred gallons of T.V.O. in a tank, balanced on old railway sleepers stood nearby.

'Teddy' was to prove a reluctant starter, especially on cold, frosty, winter mornings. Temperamental to say the least, one had to have the throttle slightly opened, ignition just right, make sure the last drop of paraffin had been drained out of the carburettor from the day before. Turn the petrol switch on, make sure it was petrol coming through by letting some run over your fingers, sniff it, "Yes, that's O.K." "Let's give him a try!" Push the starting handle down, round and smartly up. It takes all my strength, "Bugger, the engines stiff this morning." I try again, after advancing the throttle another notch, this time he fired once. Again, time after time, I swing the handle, he kicks back, got to watch out, that handle can break your wrist, flying back like that! "What's the matter with the sodding thing this morning?"

I remove the four champion plugs, sure enough two are badly oiled up, dismantle the trouble makers, wipe dry, scrape off the black carbon deposits with my pocket knife, set the points, replace three plugs, the fourth is connected but left lying on top of the engine block, giving the handle a swing I can check to see if there is a spark. "Yes, that's O.K." One seldom got trouble with the Bosch magneto.

With everything back in place the first swing on the handle and the engine burst into life, ticking over sweet as a nut on petrol. A canvas blind on the front of the radiator was kept in place until the engine was warm enough to be switched over to T.V.O.

I taught myself to plough with tractor and the two furrow international. To watch a skilled ploughman strike a straight furrow across a field, then make a leisurely return, turning over fresh, damp soil providing a rich meal of worms and grubs for hundreds of rooks and seagulls, it looks so easy, but it was to take a long time before I mastered the art. On reasonable going, three acres a day was the norm. It took fifteen gallons of T.V.O. and 'Teddy' needed almost a gallon of engine oil as well! £1 per acre was the normal charge for contract ploughing. My new outfit turned a fair few acres over the years for neighours, but it was a hard days work to earn three pounds and pay for fuel at a 1/- a gallon out of that! Certainly, not a quick road to riches.

Moving from farm to farm along public roads was a real bind. Heavy wooded blocks had to be bolted on the iron rear wheels between the spade lugs to protect the road surface. When eventually fitted and ready for the road one still had to drive painfully slow, and at journey's end, off had to come the blocks once more.

I did a lot of tractor work for John A. Betts. Cultivating, harrowing, ridging for potatoes. Ploughing on his high land above Hampstead Norreys on winter days was damned cold work. No airconditioned, safety cabs equipped with radio and cassette players in those days! Icy, windswept rain beat across the open landscape, spade-lugs bit into frozen ground. There's a nasty jolt as the ploughshare strikes a large hidden flint, bucking like an unbroken two year old. I made a primitive cab. A wooden frame attached to the mudguard supports and draped with West of England hessian sacks, which helped to keep out the worst of the driving rain. On really frosty days, despite dressing up as though a trip to the North Pole was planned, sitting hours on end on that iron sprung seat was not pleasant. Hands and feet were in danger of frostbite. On a flat field I soon discovered that I could dismount and walk alongside whilst ploughing holding the steering wheel with a piece of rope, keeping the front wheel against the furrow wall. One had to be a bit of an athlete to get back on board before the unmanned tractor hit the boundary fence though!!

Disaster struck one frosty morning, an accident that almost cost me my life. I had contracted to plough fifteen acres on Fisher's farm and then to work down a seed bed for spring barley. The ploughing was finished, the tractor and cultivator left in the field overnight; after helping Dad milk I snatched a quick breakfast before walking across the fields taking with me some sandwiches for lunch break and a five gallon can of T.V.O.

Teddy hated cold mornings, but after the usual struggle he burst into life, we were soon away down the field, the spring-tined cultivator breaking down the frost encrusted furrows. On a gentle slope, there was no fence or hedge at the bottom, the field was separated from the next by a twelve foot deep ravine cut in the sandy soil over many years by running water. Overgrown by briars, hawthorn, elder, long grass and weeds, it made a good windbreak and cover for wildlife. Now the only brake a standard Fordson can boast, is that when one pushed the clutch to the footplate with your right foot, in theory it put the tractor out of gear and acted as a brake. A metal hook was provided to hold the pedal down, which then served as the handbrake.

Anyway, I didn't need a brake, my tractor was pulling a six foot wide cultivator. Reaching the bottom headland I turned to the left. Not having a diff-lock which one gets on modern tractors, Teddy turned only slightly still continuing mainly in a forward direction, the fully locked front wheels pushing sideways through the loose sandy soil. Putting my weight on the clutch, I endeavoured to take it out of gear. It was jammed solid, we still continued forward towards the ravine. Pushing the clutch pedal down to its fullest extent. This should have applied the brake and stopped the tractor. But because it was such a cold morning, and the oil thick, the brakes failed to work.

It all happened in a few seconds, I was standing up striving to turn away from the edge of the ravine, foot-brake full on to no avail. Teddy moved relentlessly forward, too late to abandon ship, I knew he was going over, one cannot get off over the side as he tips, you go with it to end up dead underneath. Later I was to discover that on the opposite bank from where I went over grew the only tree of any size down the length of that ditch. An old pollard oak in fact. As the tractor went over, cultivator still attached, I grappled an overhanging branch, it bent, but held. I was yanked from the seat and saved from certain death. My tractor landed completely upside down, wheels still spinning, steam hissing out of the radiator. To this day I cannot remember whether I walked to Fisher's Farm, or home across the fields. I was very shocked. My main concern was that poor old Teddy had had it, he couldn't survive that treatment.

The next day a crane from town lifted the wreck out of the swirling muddy water, putting it back on four wheels once more. The upright exhaust had been broken off, all the oil in the sump had drained into the cylinders. Back home and clean again, I replaced fuel, oil and water, swung the starting handle and he fired first time, none the worst apparently for the 'ass over tip adventure'!

I had to remove the mudguards to knock them into some sort of shape again, for the rest of his days, Teddy bore the scars where steel spade-lugs had pierced his wings! After that I always worked with a wider headland, keeping well clear of pits and ditches!

We still continued working the horses until the early 1950's, but right through the war years, in fact until 1955, our faithful Standard Fordson was Dad's only mechanical power for field work. Eventually 'Teddy' was sold to Mr Pope of Cold Ash Farm for £45. It was a sad day seeing him chug down the farm-road, black smoke fouling the atmosphere. It was like losing an old friend. My young sons Michael and Tony had their first tractor rides sitting on the wide mud-guards. I hoped the new owner treated the tractor with care, not expecting it to pull too much – 'Teddy' no longer had the guts in his engine like in the early days at Mousefield!

When Farmer Pope moved to Aston Turrill, Teddy went too. I often wondered what happened to him in the end. Did he end his days on the scrap heap, or maybe even now lies rusting away behind a barn amongst the stinging nettles? Perhaps he was lucky and now resides carefully restored to former glory in some agricultural museum – I'm sure I would recognise 'Teddy' at once if I saw him!

More Stories From Newbury's Livestock Market

Newbury's livestock market held a great fascination for me. A quaker burial ground in the distant past, sales had been held there over a very long period. The first reference to a cattle market in Newbury was made in 1843 but it is certain one existed long before that. Finally closing on 26th June 1969, the site is now a multi-storey car park, even that is to be demolished shortly for some new development.

However, I like to remember it as it was in the days when the local farmers and their wives came to town on market day, a bustle of activity. Auctioneers and their porters working flat out to get stock into their allocated pens. A drover, wielding a spoon-like piece of wood, smeared a patch of thick glue on a cows rump and slapped a ticket with the lot number which had to correspond with the clerk's list of owners.

The professional cattle drovers were a motley crowd, all had a distinct character of their own. Mostly dressed in ill-fitting trousers, caked with a decade of cow manure, these were held in place by a thick, wide leather belt or a length of cord. Broad hairy chests exposed by a buttonless shirt open at the neck, beneath which was a very grubby vest, changed perhaps once a year and certainly slept in every night! Some would sport an old waistcoat held together across a large belly by a single button. Even wire nails can replace buttons if the owner is without a wife!!! Various headgear shaded weather beaten faces of men that spent most of their lives in the open air, travelling from market to market, farm sale to fairground, driving livestock any distance across country. One of their few possessions a well used ash or hazel stick, cut from some hedgerow, some preferred a disused drain rod. This supple bamboo cane wrapped with black tape or twine around the top giving a good hand grip, the bottom split and broken from much use. They all had some nick-name that suited their particular character. Even in my early market days the

R.S.P.C.A. Inspector kept a close watch on too heavy use of the stick when driving cattle, but this didn't prevent much cursing and swearing to get stock into the Sale Ring. Cattle would be walked around the ring whilst bidding progressed. If a drover knew that a drink (luck money) may be passed his way from a satisfied seller, he was adept at showing off a bunch of cattle to the best advantage, keeping the worst beast in the centre where it could not easily be seen! Dad always hired a Mr Clarke, whom everyone knew as 'Clarkie', at Newbury Market. He was superb at his trade, but expensive, he needed an awful lot of 'topping up'.

At the end of the auction, buyers, sellers, drovers, auctioneers, and their staff all made a bee-line for the New Inn, now long since demolished. This public house had a licence extension on market day until 4 pm. Dad was a teetotaller, but we sometimes went into the bar lounge to find a client or collect some money. I was always amazed at the amount of drink, especially whisky, that was consumed. The hum of conversation filled the room, air heavy with cigar and cigarette smoke. Buxom bar-maids in revealing low-cut dresses served endless pints of beer. Few customers paid for their drinks, I presumed that it was being marked up on the slate of some of the wealthier farmers, many of whom had an enormous capacity for liquid refreshments!!! The pub on Market Day was a noisy place. Roars of rapturous laughter from one corner of the room where some wit had cracked a particularly good joke to the liking of the company. Another group in serious discussion on new fangled farming methods. There would still be deals being struck, a dealer often re-sold a bunch of store cattle or a flock of gimmers he had purchased earlier in the auction, before the main body of buyers had arrived. "Didn't 'alt to sell 'im, only doing it to help a friend mind, probably have to pay more for the same stock next wick."

Quite a number of cattle would be sent off to new destinations by rail – driven out of Market Street, turning right up Cheap Street, and thence to the G.W.R. Station, there in-pounded in massive pens made of disused railway sleepers, strong enough to hold the largest bull. Special cattle trucks shunted alongside, into which the bellowing animals were loaded, soon to be on their way to various parts of the country. Dairy cows, in-calf and bulling heifers going to the lush grasslands of the West Country. A large proportion purchased by a Mr Albert Whitehead, a well-known cattle dealer from Castle Cary in Somerset. My grandfather, Mr Jack Perris and his son, sold cattle

to this man every week. Many beef stores travelled north on the Didcot Line, heading for the rich grazing grounds of the Midlands.

Sheep numbers had declined drastically in the 1930's in the Newbury District, the numbers auctioned in the market remained low. Pigs, mainly Berkshires and their crosses, always had a good showing. Auctioneers of that period were Mr Stephen Hagger, Frank Neate, to be followed a little later by Collin and Desmond Barton, Fred Coles and John Pallet. There were many others, but I cannot remember their names. Well-known livestock buyers, Ivan Snook, Douglas Ponting, Basil Povey, Geff Ryman, Bill Liddiard, Mr Walvyn, Albert Whitehead. The Randall Bros., Coles the Butcher, J.C. Perris, Bimbo Payne, and of course, Frank Houghton.

An interesting corner of the old market was the poultry section. Presented for sale were hundreds of dozens of new laid eggs. Definitely all free range!! In spring time settings of fertile eggs purchased for hatching out under broody hens.

Rabbits, dead and alive, pheasants in season, guinea pigs, ferrets in boxes poke their pink nostrils through fine mesh wire, bantams, ducks, old hens for killing, point of lay pullets and innumerable boxes of day-old chicks. The usual crowd of buyers and on-lookers, surrounded the auctioneer as he moved from pen to pen with his endless gabble.

With the approach of Christmas, there would be plenty of plump turkeys, capons, ducks and geese on offer. Local farmers, publicans, and country people with an acre or two of grass or fruit orchard, found geese useful to keep the grass under control. These garrulous birds made excellent watch dogs with their loud hissing and aggressive nature. Geese can be driven quite well in a flock, and I can remember, in my youth, seeing a gaggle of geese being walked into town on market day, a noisy procession, but orderly. They would have their feet dipped in some sticky substance, then covered with sand, this was to prevent their feet getting rubbed raw on hard roads.

The years passed by, market days came and went, Dad sold his cattle or sheep, I bought some pigs, or a few calves. We seldom missed a Thursday Auction except during the War Years. Newbury and its market day was changing. With the decade of the 30's coming to an end, there was now little horse transport, farmers were getting more affluent. This period was the hey day of our local market, but the War brought great changes. When peace at last returned to Europe, there was a brief spell of prosperity, but the market site was far too small to accommodate the ever increasing size of transport lorries, access into the town centre was difficult, pens were too small and outdated. The auctioneers and staff tried, but the writing was on the wall, and like so many other country towns, Newbury was to lose its livestock market.

The post-war years of Newbury Market gave farmers stable prices, and they enjoyed a reasonable degree of prosperity although we still found much to grumble about. In 1948 store pigs realised three to four pounds each, a porker ten pounds. Dad purchased an in-calf shorthorn heifer for £21, and a cross-bred cow and calf also for £21.

Five years later, store pigs made £6 to £7 each, with porkers at £15. Although I note that Dad purchased a cow for £11-10-0, I can't imagine she'd filled many churns of milk!

The decade of the 60's heralded a continuous decline in throughput at the market. With stock numbers dropping, buyers attended other larger centres. Hauliers found it unprofitable to make a journey to market with only half a load. Towards its final days I was driving a blue painted Ford cattle truck, with which I transported two full loads, the entire dairy herd, to market for Mr Terry Deacon of Curridge. The milch cows, freshly calved or close to calving, made between fifty and eighty-five pounds each.

That day I purchased two of them, one in the auction cost me eighty pounds on the fall of the hammer. A smart looking young Friesian cow due with her second calf in two weeks, she had all the signs of coming with a good udder. Despite the fact that this small herd disposal had been well advertised, there were few buyers round the ring that day. Plenty of onlookers, but a scarcity of farmers with cheque books willing to spend money. Terry, looking more and more dejected refused to sell at the price offered, what he considered the best cow in his herd. "She's not to go for a penny less than one hundred pounds" he shouted across the ring to the auctioneer, Fred Coles. The last genuine bid had been ninety pounds. "We can't get up there today, I've got no chance with this tight-fisted lot, let her walk. Well, that's it, gentlemen," explained Fred, "your last chance to purchase first class dairy cows at this auction." And indeed it was, the date being June 26th 1969. The last sale of livestock to be held in Newbury Cattle Market.

The crowd quickly dispersed, breaking up into small groups to gossip about the market closure. Most agreed it had been inevitable: "Auctioneers didn't give a damn about the place, didn't look after their customers," seemed to be the general comment. Most of the farmers seemed to bemoan the fact that they would now have to travel to Reading or Chippenham to sell or buy stock. "Take all day, and who wants to go to market on a Saturday when we be all short of labour, bloody stupid day to hold a sale, I say!"

After the sale I had gone to wash out my cattle lorry. I found it best to wait until the other drivers had finished their vehicles. There were only two hosepipes and not really enough water pressure to get a good jet out of both. I was busy cleaning down when Terry Deacon came up the rear tailboard. "Come to give me a hand then, Terry?" I enquired. "No, I was wondering if you wanted to buy that cow of mine, what I didn't sell. My best cow, you know, give over five a day when her calves in, quiet as a mouse she is, and milks out like a silk glove. It's her third calf and she's due to the Hereford, that calf could be wo'th fifteen quid if its a bull." "I didn't mean to take a penny less than a hundred quid, but you can take her for ninety. I won't have to pay auction if I sell her to you." Poking the rubber water hose out through the lorry ventilator flap I stopped washing down. I suppose I should make him an offer, I thought to myself. She was a good cow, and would give plenty of milk, there was no such thing as milk quotas in those days.

"Well, Terry, tell you what I'll do; you owe me twenty pounds for the two loads into Market today. I will give you sixty pounds, take the cow, and pay you now." Shaking his head, Terry replied: "Come on, give us seventy pounds and we call it quits, your transport's dear, it's only three or four miles into market from Curridge you know." It's my turn to say something. "Look, I'll split the difference, make it sixty-five pounds, we'll load her up and settle up right now." "Alright," said Terry, "You are a hard man, Bert, but I don't want to take her back again, can't get the milking machine out everyday for one cow!"

Those two cows turned out well, both calved in with Hereford cross bull calves and remained in our small herd at Mousefield for many years.

On that last auction sale in Newbury Market, Charles Moore sent in the one and only pen of store pigs. Nine weeks old, the eight blue and white large black cross large white weaners occupied the corner pen under the wall.

I had made up my mind that I was going to purchase the last lot of pigs to be auctioned in Newbury Market. As it turned out, there was little competition and the hammer came down at six pounds, two shillings each. "Bert Houghton is the buyer" called out Collin Barton in his usual business-like voice. The little crowd of farmers and onlookers didn't fully comprehend that this was the end of an era. The last livestock to be sold by auction in the town of Newbury except for poultry, and a few rabbits.

"What would I do on a Thursday now between milkings? Could stay home on the farm, always plenty of jobs to be done. The place would look a little tidier if I spent more time on it!"

Nevertheless I was rather sad. I had enjoyed my local market for so many years. Father and I had done thousands of pounds worth of business on that two acre corner of the town, made a few pounds and lost a few, but more important, we had made many friends and very few enemies.

My Father had made for himself a good name in the locality, he was highly respected for honest dealing and promptly paid his bills.

Always prepared to listen patiently to other people's problems, his counsel was ever in demand. I have always tried to follow his example, perhaps with limited success. Hopefully my sons will do the same!!!

On reflection, I wonder, do the ghosts of those old drovers and farming characters flit around the market site on dark, moonless nights, to meet once more in the New Inn. Smite huge gnarled hands over some clinched cattle deal and tip up their flagons of ale amidst rombustious laughter? After all, we must remember, the site was once a cemetery!!

Cattle Dealing

My father had taken to buying and selling livestock to augment the income he made from his small dairy herd. He did a lot of business with a certain Mr Richardson who had a large grazing farm on the Berkshire Downs. His farmhouse and buildings nestle in the centre of the village of Chilton, and his son Bob still farms there today.

This business associate of my Father's was a big powerful character, broad shouldered, with hands as large as spades, and a hearty, infectious laugh. Renowned for his own special brand of 'Perry', a very strong brew made from pears. The Showering Brothers of Somerset made a fortune from this drink, gave it some sparkle and called it Babycham.

Mr Richardson made frequent visits to farms and sales in Ireland where he purchased Irish store cattle, shipping them back to graze on the open downs. Now that I had left school I accompanied my Father on his buying trips. Dad had purchased a red-painted Model-T Ford van, morning milking over, we set off.

The road, now called the A34, took us through the village of Beedon, then down the narrow main street of East Ilsley, once famous for its sheep fairs. Then it wends its way up and over one of the highest points of the Berkshire Downs before dropping down to by-pass Chilton. We carried a reserve two gallon can of petrol strapped to the running board and a container of water for the radiator in case the old girl boiled going up a hill. We made frequent stops if the weather was warm to let the engine cool down. On arriving at Chilton Farm, Mr Richardson could usually be found in the yard, making himself busy, but at the same time keeping one eye on the approach road for his prospective customers. Dad at the wheel, we swing into the cobbled farmyard, a wisp of steam swirling up from the brass radiator, a sigh of relief, we'd made it.

Bob strides over to meet us with a huge smile on his face, arm outstretched to shake Dad's hand in a vice like grip: "Hello Frank, nice to see you again" and to me "morning me boy. Have you both had a good journey?" Without waiting for an answer, he said

"Com'on in lets get you boys something to drink." Once inside the big farmhouse kitchen he goes to his well stocked drink cupboard and out came a large bottle of perry. "You'll like this Frank, set you up for the rest of the day" he said pouring out two big glass fulls and a smaller amount for me. "Cheers" as we raised our glasses. "I've got some grand cattle to show you two this morning," says Bob. "Here come on, drink up, I've got plenty more of this stuff." He tops Dad's glass to the brim. Now we soon learnt that the real object of this hospitality was to get his intended purchaser into as good a mood as possible. Ply him with as much perry as he could consume. Bob himself was immune to the effects. "Come on then you chaps, lets go and see these cattle. I've got the best lot of stirks I've had in many a long day." Out in the yard once more we piled into his old cross-country Rover car and having made sure the cattle were on the furthest part of his land he drove hell for leather across the downs, following a very rough farm track, through great ruts of mud and water, and up over a humped-back bridge, crossing the Newbury/ Didcot railway-line. By the time we got to the meadow where the cattle grazed, our driver had made sure the perry was well and truly shook up and hopefully one would be carefree about parting with ones money!

My father always maintained that the first time he had this treatment, he remembers getting out of the car and carefully picking his feet well up over non-existing long grass!! This time Dad was quite sober. My head was swimming a bit but I had only come along for the ride. Twenty-five grand roan shorthorn heifers gazed curiously at the approaching vehicle, coming to a halt we all got out. "Com'on, com'on, com'on then." Bob calls in a deep voice. They mill round us as we stroll among them. Dad turns each one with his stick, casting a knowledgeable eye over every heifer, looking especially to see if they have the making of a good udder. Pointing one out, Dad says "That one's bit smaller and thinner than the rest." "Just a mite younger, that's all, Frank, nothing wrong with her. I'll stand up to any on 'em, they're all right and straight."

We give each one a good look over. "Yes, I think they will do my job, but what are you asking for them, that's the next question," says Dad. "£15 a piece" says our farmer friend, knowing full well he's well over the top of their true value. "If that is what you really mean, we will not be having a deal today" says Dad. Bob tries to look disappointed, but he's an old hand at dealing. "What's your price then, Frank?" "Ten pounds a piece would be nearer the mark" my Father replies. "That's no good, no good at all, you knows a bunch of bullers like these are worth pounds more, you won't find another lot of heifers like these in Berkshire."

By now the cattle have put their heads down, wandered off, quietly grazing, oblivious of the two men and a boy discussing their future. Bob, who always carried a big forked thumb-stick, strode off and gently drove them back to where we stood.

"Tell you what I'll do, I'm trying hard to meet you, fourteen apiece, you chaps got yourselves a good deal there." Dad would now say, "Look, I'll make it eleven pounds each, how about it?" "No good Frank, no good at all, sorry to drag you two all this way for nothing, but I always likes to see you, even if we don't have a deal." Silence reigns for a few moments. Bob suddenly stands almost aggressively in front of Dad, blocking his path with his massive frame, his left hand reached for Dad's right, at the same time raising his own right hand ready to strike their two palms together. The traditional way to clinch a bargain, no written agreements were ever required in those days. "Frank, I'm going to try once more, thirteen pounds apiece, I know thirteen is unlucky but only for me, com'on, don't be so bloody hard." Dad shakes his head, "No, can't be done I'm afraid. We shall have to leave them today. Pity, would have liked to have had a deal with you, but we must get back to the farm, and get on our way now, we've got a long journey to do." We climb aboard the old Rover, and at a much more leisurely pace retrace our wheelmarks down the old car track.

Cattle and prices are not mentioned again on our return to the farm. We make as if to leave when Bob says: "Want a cup-of-tea before you get on our way?" "Sounds a good idea" Dad replies. We follow him into the kitchen. "Put the kettle on Mother" Bob says to his buxom wife. "Like getting blood out of a stone, trying to sell cattle to these two today. They ain't got their buying boots on that's for sure." Still showing no further interest in the cattle, we don't mention them again. We enjoy a good brew, I make short work of a few home-made rock cakes. Outside again, Dad gets into our van, retards the ignition by means of the control lever on the steering column, advances the throttle a few notches. I unstrap the starting handle, give it a brisk turn, and the engine fires first time. Dad revs the engine, I get in the passenger seat. Bob seemed most concerned that we were really leaving, and he hadn't taken our money, my father could certainly put on a good act. Mr Richardson puts his hairy, bronzed arm on the open van window, leans inside, with desperation in his voice saying: "Look I don't want you going off without buying these heifers, I'm going to try again – £12-10-0 a piece and that's final."

Now after two or three hours of small talk, bluff and counter bluff, the business gets serious. Now its Dad's turn: "I'm going to give you twelve pounds apiece, please yourself Bob. I shan't give anymore if we stay here all day." "You're a hard man Frank, I hope you don't bring this son of yorn up so tight-fisted." "Come on", he reaches for Dad's hand, "we'll split the difference. This time their two palms smack together. Twenty-five red and roan shorthorn heifers change hands at twelve pounds, five shillings each. Total sum of £306-5-0, a large sum of money, and a very big deal for my father to make. We step out into the cobbled yard once more, we hadn't intended going anyway! Out came the cheque book: "Got a pen Bob?" "Just a minute" he replies, "there's one in the kitchen if the kids haven't pinched it. Almost running he disappears indoors, coming out a few minutes later holding it up triumphantly. "Here you are Frank." A cheque is written out on the van bonnet, and handed over. Bob surveys it carefully. Satisfied and with a smile on his face at last, he booms, "When you going to fetch 'em then Frank?" "Do you want me to rail 'em to ya, taint far into Didcot station, the whole lot would go on two trucks?" "No, thanks" replies Dad, "It would mean we'd have to de-truck at Newbury Station, then walk 'em all through the town, whilst we're doing that, we may as well walk 'em over the downs, they seem a quiet bunch." "Oh yes, they'll walk alright. Been used to being driven about." "Me and my son will help you on the first mile or so." "Can you give us a week to get things organised our end" asked Dad. "Sure, no longer though, I'm not overflushed with grass on these poor ole downs." "Do fine. Next Monday morning then?" "Bout ten o'clock if alls well" says Dad.

For quite a few previous years my Father had supplied shorthorn bulling heifers to John A. Betts, Manor Farm, Hampstead Norreys, and Mr Cyril Dewe of Everington Farm. Both large dairy farmers. During the following week Dad and I made it our business to drive over to see these customers of ours. Both these farmers accepted Dad at his word, Father had a good name in the district for fair dealing. The price was set at fifteen pounds apiece delivered to their farms. A useful profit would be made but first we had to get them there.

The following Monday morning we made an early start after milking our cows. Dad, myself and a farmworker we employed, called Jack Little, setting off over the downs by horse and float. We couldn't take the Ford. It would be inconvenient at the other end. Arriving at Chilton Farm the cattle would be bellowing in the yard, collected up and ready to travel. A quick cup of tea before we set off, no time to waste today. Opening the yard gate, the cattle came out with a rush, setting off at a steady trot. Dad riding up front with Black Beauty and the float, myself and young Bob Richardson on either flank. Jack bringing up the rear. Bob senior struggled to keep up, after a few hundred yards he bellowed to Dad up front: "Guess you'll be alright now Frank, they'll soon settle down, good luck, give us a shout when you be wanting some more." Milling and bellowing, our charges left ample evidence of their passing, as we made our way down the village street. Some of the villagers came out anxiously shutting their garden gates. Two miles on our way. Now the road starts to climb up and over the Berkshire Downs – the cattle had by now got a lot steadier and caused us no trouble, giving me time to admire the vast solitude of those rolling hills, quiet and peaceful in Spring or Summer. Cattle grazed on either side, looking in our direction, they came running to the boundary fence, mooing and calling to these new faces, following our herd till they could go no further. Larks soared skywards with their musical song. Few travellers passed our way. Perhaps a horse and wagon with the carter taking a load of dung to an outlying pasture, another traveller passing through by horse and buggy, someone walking over the downs to the next village. An occasional motor car, its driver forced to stop to allow our herd to pass. Sometimes we had to keep our charges on the wide grass verge to permit a lorry free passage. Having passed Buffalow Bill's cabin at the foot of the downs, the driver would drop down into first gear to grind his way to the top, transporting his heavy load from the midlands to Southampton docks. It is hard to imagine what chaos would be caused today if one attempted to drive twenty-five head of cattle on the A34!!!

Once our herd was moving quietly, more tired now as we got nearer home, I could drop behind to walk with Jack, if the roadside was well fenced. Never any question of riding in the float. Crossing open ploughed land I walked the headland preventing our herd from straying, and at the same time my instructions from Father was to keep my eyes open for discarded horse shoes, plough shares, and

land-sides, this would be placed in the float and later added to a slowly growing pile of scrap iron back at home. All to be sold just before Christmas. The money used to buy us some oranges, bananas, and nuts. My parents were careful with their money – it didn't come easy!!!

Haymaking and Rick Building

With a dairy herd and young stock on the farm, which all had to be fed through each long winter, hay making was an important job for all the family. Taking up most of our labours through June and July. We didn't make silage until after the War. 'Dunged' in the autumn, Dad would 'shut up' two or three of his best meadows. These would be chain harrowed and rolled in the spring, and we would start mowing from mid-June if the weather looked settled. Chain harrows in Dad's case often consisted of a long metal pole from which dragged large black thorn bushes sometimes weighted down with a heavy length of timber strapped on top. This was pulled by one of the horse team, and was usually my job. Despite working the field both ways it did little more than rake down the mole heaps and scatter the cow pats!

A few years later, I persuaded my father to mechanise the chain harrowing. He purchased a Rover car for seven pounds ten shillings, and a second-hand chain harrow at a farm sale, for three pounds. After that each meadow got a thorough rake out, every sprig of moss pulled out, every mole heap flattened.

If we got a wet June, it meant the hay harvest couldn't start until after the turn of the days, 21st June, Dad's birthday. "It will clear up now, you see if it don't" he would confidently declare; and sure enough, he was often right. A late start meant, of course, that work on the hay would drag on into August. Dad sharpened up the knives on a specially constructed wooden stand. With one of his heavy hob-nailed boots holding the table steady, he'd lean over the stand, and with long precise strokes of the file, put the right angled edge on each section. In those days we had a Bamford mowing machine pulled by two horses.

Dad often rose at 4 a.m., harnessed the team, and start mowing soon after. Grass cuts better when dew rests heavy in the hayfield. Working alone, man and his two horses, with just the larks, fieldfares and crows for company, swathes of mature, natural grass fell before the agitating mower knife which rattled between the fingers of the machine. Recently made mole heaps could be a bugbear, quickly blunting a sharp knife, or worse, small stones could get wedged, resulting in broken sections which had to be replaced.

Round and round the meadow; Dad rode behind his two faithful horses, sitting on an iron seat, padded with a little sack of hay. With each rotation, the patch of uncut grass became smaller, the early cut swathes already wilting in the sun, as it climbed higher in the sky. Scared rabbits finally broke cover, us lads, armed with stout sticks and with the assistance of a good dog, would give chase with wild whoops. Few rabbits made it to the boundary hedge.

Dad and I made the rick bottom, bundles of brushwood called buffers, or bavens, were used to make a foundation on which was placed a layer of clean straw. This was to keep the valuable fodder off the damp ground. Dad would look at his crop and from long experience, assess how many wagon loads there were in the meadow. Four pegs were driven into the ground, representing the corners of the rectangular rick, ten, maybe twelve, by six yards, taken to a reasonable height, this size would accommodate a twenty ton crop of hay. A heavy yield off ten acres.

I never liked making hay in Well Meadow. Both men and horses were plagued with horse flies, vicious black insects, with a sting that caused a nasty swelling, and days of irritation. If the weather looked to be set fine, Dad would instruct me to get up the hayfield and turn the crop. "Get the sun on t'other side." We had a martins machine which turned the swathes over, but I can remember even into the nineteen fifties, turning small acreages of grass by hand, with a wood tined hay rake.

The following day one of the horses was reversed and harnessed between the shafts of a ten foot wide Lister hayrake. The hay, wilting in the heat of the midday sun, was raked into windrows. Once the cut grass had been moved, Dad wouldn't chance the weather for too long, all the family, plus any outside help we could muster, set to work with our long, two-pronged forks building the long rows of crisp, mellow hay into well shaped, domed cocks, each one standing some four or five feet high. When well raked down each side, these would shed all but the heaviest rain storms. Left in the meadow to mature for a week or more, standing there in silent rows awaiting horse and wagons.

Haymaking was hard, heavy, manual work, a family and social affair. Men that worked in other trades came evenings and weekends to lend a hand and earn some extra money. Everyone seemed to enjoy the work, and tea in the hayfield was an extra bonus. I look back with a certain amount of nostalgia, those days will never return, we don't even make hay these days, just round baled silage, with tractors and sophisticated machines doing all the work!

The hay pitchers came, Will Adnams, Maurice Little, some of the Staplehorns, strong men with long shaft pitching forks. It was a skilled craft, they would spit on their weather worn hands before hoisting aloft a great pitch of wellmade hay. As a young lad my job was to lead the horse and wagon between the haycocks, waiting in rows to be transported to the rick, which was already taking shape. Jack, our carter, built the load, telling the pitchers where to place each forkfull. A pitch on each corner, then fill the middle to tie it all on. Not easy material to handle, loose hay. Strike the prong well down into the cock of hay, keep the right hand close to the fork, then using the left arm and making full use of the long ash handle, one used it as a lever to swing a real good pitch up onto the wagon. As the load got higher, it needed considerable strength and expertise to place it just where required. "'Old tight!" I had to shout each time we moved on. If I forgot, or the horse jigged on a bit, there came a roar from above, "What you think you be doing, boy, you'll have me arse ore tip, if you bent more careful!"

Dad sometimes borrowed another horse and wagon from his neighbour, Fred Kimber, at Cold Ash Farm. This meant his workman 'Old Charlie' came too. The trouble was nobody could ever do anything right for him. "Look you, this is how we does the job up at our place!" was one of his oft repeated statements. Or: "That hay 'ent fit to stack, her'll fire within a month, you mark my words." If hay is stacked before being well made in catchy weather, it can catch fire some six weeks later from internal combustion.

With two wagons or even three, if we had the labour, one would be unloading at the rick, one filling up out in the field, and a third travelling out empty or returning full. I would leave one horse standing patiently at the rick, change over, and go back out with another one. Dad built the rick, that was his job, he trusted no one else to do it. With much skill, learnt over many years of practice, the finished model was something of great pride to him. Leaning slightly outwards up to the eaves, the roof then sloped gently inwards to the top. It was not possible to pitch hay from the wagon to the roof of the rick, on those later stages, some small person, which was usually myself, was placed in the pitch hole, a difficult, dirty job, passing hay on up to the rickbuilder high above. One got enough hayseeds in your hair, in your eyes, up your nose, and down your neck to plant an acre a day!

Over two or three seasons Dad patiently taught me rick building. Both hay and corn ricks. First build a stack in the centre, working outwards to the sides, with hay place a good pitch on the corner, one more pitch either side, then tie it on with a forkfull just behind those three. Working backwards, anti-clockwise, you tied each forkfull on, like roofing tiles. 'Always keep the middle full, that's the secret," Dad impressed upon me. "If you don't yer corners will slip, and you'll end up wiv' policemen standing round, then whot'll neighbours think on us? Fine lot of rick builders those Houghtons be!" If a haystack started to slip on corner or side, long stout poles were cut from the wood, and an attempt made to prevent the whole lot falling over. Hence the name of policemen, as policemen can hold up traffic, so they could hold up a rick!!

It took skill and judgement, plus years of experience to complete a large hayrick and finish the job with the correct quantity of material. It would be useless to get, say up to the eaves, and your carter to come back from the field and say: "That's it, boss, no more out there sides a bit ole rakings." In which case one couldn't complete the roof of your rick. Alternatively, to find, as one was putting the finishing touches to a grand job, that there were still six wagon loads out on the ground. "Were be gowin to put rest on it governor" said our carter with a smirk on his face. There was a certain leeway in the fact that if there was a larger crop than anticipated, you could make an extra course round your rick before commencing building the roof. There was however a limit to how high you can build. This was determined by the fact that a man could only pitch the height of his prong.

The advent of the mechanised elevator gave more scope and certainly made rick-building a less laborious task, but we didn't own one until the early days of the War.

With the hay harvest safely gathered in, our ricks standing proud in the yard, they would be allowed to 'settle and sweat for a spell'. If the grass had been stacked a bit on the green side, because of catchy weather, Dad would keep an anxious eye on them, looking out as soon as the sun rose, he'd return to the house, looking worried and saying to Mum, "Them ricks be 'piping' up fairish smarn'in, lets hope they don't fire, should have waited another day or two 'fore we stacked. Them blasted weather men, no good listening to 'em. They just say whatever comes into their 'eads, then rush on 'ome to breakfast, and lets us get on wi'it. Bet they laughs their heads off if the sun comes out after they said twere gowin to rain. I'll back me own judgement next time round."

Ten days had passed, the little swirls of steam gently rising to greet the dawn had subsided, we could barely see them now. Dad was more cheerful: "Those ricks be alright Mother. Shan't have to call the fire brigade after all." In fact we never in my time had a rick catch fire, but it was quite a common occurrence in the district.

When our ricks had settled, we would 'tuck' them. That meant starting at the eaves and working downwards, plucking all the loose hay out, to leave a firm smooth side. This was then collected in small heaps, I would then climb our longest ladder, carrying a pitch of hay up to the apex to 'cap 'er off'. This was followed by a few pitches of loose straw, and our rick was now ready for thatching. We always had a rick of threshed wheat straw left over from the previous harvest.

Now came what I considered the most skilled job in the farming calendar, thatching a rick. I watched and laboured many years for my father before he let me try my hand at thatching. Slowly under his guidance, I made progress, he was a very patient man, taking a lot of time and trouble to teach his son this ancient craft. My first attempts were on wheat ricks in the Autumn. Ricks that were soon to be threshed anyway, so if my unskilled work let the rain in, it didn't matter quite so much. The loose straw pulled from the stack by hand was then combed and laid in sheaves. A stout hazel stick, shaped like a large letter 'V', held six to eight of these bundles, which were then tied at the top with a cord. The whole lot hoisted onto one's shoulder to be carried up the long thatching ladder. Work started from the centre of the roof on the widest side. Commencing at the bottom with an overhang of some twelve inches, a two foot wide strip of straw was laid out, then another layer above to overlap some third of its length and so on to the top. Now with a small hand rake, which in our case was a homemade affair, just a well-shaped wooden handle with six inch nails driven through to make a useful comb, split hazel sticks were pushed into the roof of the rick at intervals. Binder twine from one peg to the next held the well combed straw in place. "Push them pegs in hard and upwards, don't want the rain to run down the stick and into the rick," Dad always impressed on me. One strip complete, come down, move the ladder over, take up more straw, lay the next layer, don't forget to tuck the second run under the first a few inches, thus sealing the join, peg down and tie with binder twine. Corners were difficult, wide at the bottom, narrow at the top.

When our rick had a bright new cap of weather-proof straw, held down firmly with pegs and ties, clipped neatly along the top and round the eaves, I stood back and admired my handiwork. I got further satisfaction when my work survived the first winter gale without a straw out of place. It always seemed a shame when the time came to take some straw off, and cut into the rick to give the cows their first autumn feed as the grass ceased to grow, and milk yields started to drop.

The hay knife, pointed but with a wide blade, was kept razor sharp. The handle at right angles to the blade, allowed the operator to thrust downwards with his full weight. Layers of sweet smelling meadow hay were then carted in the horse drawn wagon, rations enough for perhaps three days for our small dairy herd waiting hungrily in the byre.

Harvest Time

Memories of harvest time in the 1930's: To me they were such happy family occasions, everyone from toddlers to tottery grandparents were welcome to lend a helping hand. The sun always seemed to shine, rising early in the eastern sky to quickly evaporate the morning dew.

It did, of course, rain all too often, so much so that some seasons harvest dragged on into October, with stooks of oats or wheat, once with the promise of a fine, bumper harvest of excellent quality grain, now standing silent and rain soaked, with green shoots from sprouted seed, matting the long ears of grain in a tangled mass. If ever carted to a rick, at best never to be more than poor quality livestock feed. If these sheaves were ricked damp, they'd dry out by the following March, but at threshing time, clouds of unhealthy white mould rose around the workers.

Wet harvests are quickly forgotten, I like to remember the sunny ones, long hot August days with cool evenings, everyone helping to

bring the harvest home. Midday, the welcome sight of my Mother coming across the home paddock to the corn field carrying her large wicker shopping basket, piled high with refreshments, cool home-made lemon drink, cold black tea, favoured by the men, a well-baked, crusty cottage loaf, and a big hunk of tasty cheddar. If early in the harvest, we would all be out stooking, work came to a stop for an hour, whilst we sat in a circle on a few sheaves of corn. Later under the shade of half finished ricks. The farm men all carried a large clasp knife with a wide curved blade, used for all manner of farm jobs, which I won't mention here. Using their thumb as a kind of back stop, they cut off a chunk of bread from the one inch wide slice, a generous piece of cheese and an onion followed the same way between broken, tobacco stained teeth.

These men of the land never seemed to shave, they always sported a week's growth of stubble, since it never got more nor less than a quarter of an inch long; I imagine they kept it under control with scissors. Hobnailed boots with a steel toe cap, the same baggy trousers, winter and summer, hoisted a few inches off the ground by a cord tied just below the knee. A grubby, collarless shirt with rolled up sleeves, nearly always a waistcoat, was worn too, plus a wide variety of head gear. Mostly they were men of few words, quite content to spend the dinner break silently eating, apparently deep in thought. Perhaps it was because they never travelled far afield or met many people outside their own family, but they seemed to have more to say to their horses, cows or dog, than they did to their fellow workers or the boss!

At thirty-six shilling a quarter, or seven pounds ten shillings per ton, North American hard wheat was flooding the English market. Dad's wheat acreage diminished but he still grew quite a few acres of oats and barley for stock feed.

When harvest was ready, Dad sharpened his scythe with a rubber or wet stone, and cut a swathe round the ripe corn. This was to allow the horse drawn binder to cut the first round without the horses trampling the standing crop. My job was to tie this cut corn into sheaves. Mother and my young sister would draw the bonds. Twist a few stems of wheat to tie the new sheaves. If the crop was short in length we made double bonds, that is, twist the two heads together for longer length.

Dad was a craftsman with the use of a scythe in grass or grain. (His scythes are still in the garage). No matter how hard I tried, I never did match his skill. To hear the steady swish, swish of the blade as he moved forward one step at the time, strong arms rigid on the double handles, the crop to fall in a neat row at his feet. A true country scene, I wish now we had captured it in a photograph or painting, but then we never gave it a thought that farming and our way of life was to undergo such drastic changes in the years ahead. Now one man sits in the air conditioned cab of a giant combine harvester, surrounded by an array of levers and dials. Red lights flash if fuel or oil gets low, another tells him when the grain tank is full. He doesn't get his hands dirty and a radio is standard equipment! A tractor and trailer draws alongside whilst still on the move to accept the flow of golden grain for transport back to the oil-fired drier and cleaner in the barn. The straw chopped, burnt or made into big bales for bedding and stock feed. This great modern combine harvester deals with five hundred acres or more each season, a far cry from the gangs of workers once required.

We had a Massey-Harris binder pulled by the two Shire Horses, one either side of the pole. This was carter Jack's job, sitting aloft on an iron seat, reins in one hand to control the horses, the other to operate a forest of levers, with a few foot pedals thrown in for luck. One lever moved the sails up, down, backwards or forwards, another to adjust where the binder twine tied the sheaf as the crop varied in height across the field. The cut corn fell onto the bed of rotating canvas which accepted it, heads to the rear and up between two more endless canvasses, thence the knotting mechanism tied neat sheaves of corn and automatically two small forks came over at the correct time to pitch each new sheaf on to cut stubble in neat rows. The clever person who invented the knotter on a binder I always thought must have been an ingenious fellow – I never did succeed in unravelling the mechanism.

On the corners both horses sometimes stopped in their tracks without command. Jack then slapped a flank with the long rein. A gruff command would urge them on in unison once more. "Com'on thur, get moving you two!" Reluctantly they'd swing round in a tight circle to the left, then round the uncut stand of grain once more, for ever getting smaller until only a small strip remained and like the hay mowing, the time had come for the rabbits to make their bolt for freedom. They had to run the gauntlet of boys, sticks and dogs. Few made it if they left it late, the scattering of hundreds of sheaves of corn and the long stubble seemed to mesmerise them. With wild whoops we gave chase as the scared bunnies darted for cover dodging from sheaf to sheaf. They are very difficult to hit with sticks, and even harder to catch.

The next job was the laborious one of stooking the sheaves of corn. Standing them up in double rows of four, six or eight. Working singly or in pairs, starting on the outside rows, we worked our way round the field. Grasp a sheaf under each arm, the long ears of grain brushing one's chin. The art of making a good stook was to thump the butt end down well on the stiff stubble leaning the ears in tight to intertwine together. The angle of the stand had to be right too, otherwise the first puff of wind would blow them over next day, and they never stood up so well the second time, apart from the fact that it meant double work. Since grain is cut earlier in the season with a binder than it is with a combine, tradition had it that the stooks had to stay in the fields whilst we heard the church bells ring three times on Sundays. If a fine dry spell set in, ours didn't stay out that long, I can tell you, Dad, seeing a neighbour get busy with horses and wagons would have to get started rickbuilding too.

Our ricks were built on staddle stones, their only use today are as ornaments in the garden. Eight or ten capped stones to a rick, then a framework of heavy timbers built criss-cross on them. On this foundation a layer of faggots or buffers as Dad called them; bundles of brushwork cut from the copse nearby. Then a layer of straw or old fusty hay, before the first load of wheat sheaves started the rick proper. In due course four to six ricks, newly thatched, would now await the hired threshing outfit.

Threshing Day

My earliest recollection of threshing days goes way back to when I was eight or nine years old. Dad hired the local contractor to thrash out his few ricks. The outfit moved in, often late afternoon, having spent the whole day packing up and moving locations. In those days the power was steam. Long before coming into view I could hear the chuff, chuff, chuff and the rattle of iron wheels on the road surface, almost as soon as the convoy passed the cemetery on the Hermitage road.

Rising the crest of Four Elms Hill (those elms vanished many years ago) I could now see the black smoke above the roadside hedge. I'm standing on the brick wall, turn and shout out in excitement "Here's the thrasher, Mum!" The whole outfit swings into our farm road, the sound reaches crescendo as the massive steam engine emerges from beneath the railway bridge, followed by the dusty threshing drum, then the straw tier, up the track in tandem, great flywheel spinning. One thing always struck me as being rather odd, and I never did find the explanation: "Why was it that the driver lavished such great care and attention on his steam engine, always oiling it, carefully wiping off the dust, polishing the beautiful brass fittings. Burnished to perfection, and yet never seemed to wash himself? Decades of soot and grime was ingrained into the skin of his face, neck, and hands.

Past our new house on the gravel track to the rick yard which was situated in the corner of what was then called 'ten acres'. Skillfully manoeuvre the threshing machine between two corn ricks, the driver and his mate then jacked up one great iron wheel, lowered another until the spirit level on its side showed the bubble dead centre. Unless rain had been forecast, Dad and Jack Little mounted the ladder and commenced removing the rick pegs, cut the string and dismantle the thatch, ready for tomorrow's early start. The whole outfit was charged on a daily basis so one didn't lose out on threshing time by not being ready to start.

It required seven or eight men and boys to run a threshing outfit at full blast. The driver came at six, cycling up the road on his old bike.

He had to stoke up and get up steam before the rest of the men came at seven o'clock. Dad was up and about early too, also the two extra men he had 'borrowed' from a neighbour for a day or two. Seven-thirty sharp the driver opened up the throttle, the engine rocked a little, black smoke puffed upwards, the long drive belt flapped as the threshing machine came to life. The vast numbers of revolving belts fascinated me, wide ones, narrow ones, some long, some short, some criss-cross, parts moved backwards and forwards. The big flywheel gathered speed, the machine began to hum, a vast cloud of choking dust erupted from the machine's innards. I remember an incident that caused quite a commotion early one winter morning. The drive belt was just setting everything in motion when one of the men flipped it off with the end of his pitching fork. "Saw sommat in the drum you" he shouted to the driver, with that there was a rattle and bang and somewhere from the machine's belly came a very scared tom cat. "Darn me, if tent a girt tabby, how the hell did he get in thur you?" Of course it had climbed in during the night, after mice.

Dad and one of his men pitched sheaves to the two men on the thresher, one deftly cut the strings retaining the cords in his hand, whilst passing the sheaf to his partner who fed the mouth of the drum. Corn flowed into West of England sacks at the back end, which kept one man busy changing sacks, wheeling away on a sack truck, and weighing them off on barn scales, 2 ¼ cwts in a sack of wheat, 2 cwts for barley, 1 ½ cwts for oats. Two hundred and fifty-two pounds was the weight of a sack of wheat and I've carried many hundreds of those monsters on my back from trailer to barn, or barn to transport lorry. Some farm men carried them like they were filled with feathers, but I was always a bit wobbly at the knees!

Shakers shook out the threshed straw either into a straw tier or loose as required, this was pitched into an elevator and a rick of thatching straw built. One dirty, dust ridden job was moving the chaff away, especially if the wind was blowing it into one's face. This job was unskilled, boy's work. After I left school, I always seemed to be allocated this unpleasant task. At the end of the day, my eyes were red-rimmed, nose choked with dust, and I'd spit black phlegm for days afterwards!

When the rick had almost reached ground level, the rats began to run. Up to now they had a warm shelter, unlimited food and safety from predators, now the day of reckoning had come. Terrier dogs, and us boys armed with stout sticks quickly despatch all but the most

nimble rats, we always made sure the bottom of our long trousers were tightly tied with string, terrified mice and rats would take refuge up one's leg! I will never forget the scream of sheer terror Alec Adnams gave one threshing day, when a huge rat run up his leg and up round his backside. "Keep still, Alec!" shouted my father, as he aimed blow after blow on the poor lad's posterior, but you cannot kill a fully grown rat like that. It wasn't many seconds before Alec whipped off his trousers, deserting his post for the rest of the day. He always kept his trousers double tied at the ankle after that experience!

The Home Guard

September 3rd 1939, saw the commencement of the Second World War. The first few months being referred to as the phoney war, when life for us country folk seemed to progress much as before, apart from minor shortages and the black out, which made driving after dark hazardous. The car's headlights blacked out except for a narrow strip of light which gave at the most some five yards visibility! As a farming family, starting work at dawn or before, seldom did the need arise to travel at night.

On the evening of Tuesday 14th May 1940, the newly appointed Secretary of State for War, Anthony Eden, spoke on the B.B.C. Home Service, as Eden explained: "I want to speak to you tonight about the form of warfare which the Germans have been employing so extensively against Holland and Belgium – namely the dropping of parachute troops behind the main defensive lines. In order to leave nothing to chance, and to supplement from sources as yet untapped the means of defence already arranged, we are going to ask you to help us in a manner which I know will be welcome to thousands of you. Since the war began the government have received countless enquiries from all over the Kingdom from men of all ages who are for one reason or another not at present engaged in military service, and who wish to do something for the defence of their country. Well, now is your opportunity. We want large numbers of such men in Great Britain, who are British subjects, between the ages of seventeen and sixty-five to come forward now and offer their services. The name of the new force which is now to be raised will be: 'The Local Defence Volunteers'. This name describes its duties in three words. This is a part-time job, so there will be no need for any volunteer to abandon his present occupation. When on duty you will form part of the armed forces. You will not be paid, but you will receive a uniform and will be armed. In order to volunteer, what you have to do is to give in your name at your local police station; and then, as and when we want you, we will let you know."

We discussed the implications of this speech next morning at breakfast. Dad said that he was far too busy to play at soldiers. If the Germans did come, he would do his bit, but in the meantime, someone had to milk the cows!

I was nineteen at the time, with no great desire to be a soldier part-time or otherwise. My mates thought it a good chance to "Have a go at Hitler!" We were the goodies, they were the baddies! 'I'll be volunteering" I announced to my parents. "More fool you" said my Mother "those Germans killed your Uncle Bert and badly wounded poor Jack. Like you they couldn't wait to get into the thick of it. There's plenty to do here on the farm, helping your father, do more good for the country than marching up and down the town with guns on your shoulders." (In the event we weren't to get guns for a long time.) In the face of this parental opposition, I did not rush to join up like thousands more, following Eden's radio announcement.

On June 17th France surrendered and Britain stood alone, we all expected the Germans to follow up their victory and shortly cross the Channel, at the same time drop thousands of parachutists to establish a foothold. I decided I would join up after the harvest, I'd have a bit more time then. Strange how I still put farming first, and invasion by a foreign power in second place. Hitler was most unlikely to delay until the end of the farming year, when it might be more convenient from our point of view! In fact we hadn't quite finished ricking our winter wheat when, about the third week in September, I cycled down to Newbury Police Station, which was adjacent to Mr Stan Hunt's farm at Speenhamland. Leaving my bike against the wall, I passed through the sand-bags that protected the station's doorway. The sergeant on duty was not over pleased to see me, having dealt with so many applicants over the last few months, however he wrote down my particulars on the standard form, which I duly signed on completion. Name and address, occupation, age etc. No questions were asked regarding physical fitness. The official requirement was that any recruit: "Must be capable of free movement" but nothing was laid down about how far or how fast.

The L.D.V. given the nickname of the 'Look, duck and vanish brigade' had been in operation for some months. It officially became known as the Home Guard on July 23rd 1940.

My papers came through a few days later. I was now a private in the Home Guard from 1st October 1940. I very much doubt that any local spies or fifth columnists reported this historic fact to Adolf

Hitler at the time. In any case it would be most unlikely to cause him any sleepless nights or to change his invasion plans!!

We had by now been given proper titles, and promised that soon we would receive a shoulder flash and cap badges of our own. A badge or rank consisted of from one to four blue stripes on the shoulders for 'Officers', and two to three chevrons on the sleeve for N.C.O.s. We received caps and denims but they were not in equal numbers, some of our members had a cap, but no uniform, or vice-versa. My slacks were far too long and I was in grave danger of tripping over my own feet. Mum cut a few inches off the bottom of the legs which improved matters somewhat, but little could be done regarding the fit of the waist. Being slim I could only keep my trousers in place by using a belt and making an overlap held with a large safety pin! Our uniforms were made of hard-wearing material, but seemed to be in two sizes only, 'Large, or very large''. If I stood still with my great coat on, it could be mistaken for an army tent!

Initially our platoon consisted of ten men under that formidable character, Sergeant Wilfred Rowles, now in his eighties, and living at 'Red Farm Gate'. Our commanding officer, a well known Brigadier of the First World War, had every intention of defending our part of West Berkshire to the last man. Meeting at Donnington Priory twice a week, a tough course of training was mapped out for us. I soon found out that serving as a soldier, even part-time was a very different occupation from farming. In particular, our leader was a great disciplinarian, and determined to turn his mixed bag of raw recruits into a resemblance of a fighting force, despite the fact that even by the late 1940's we only had two ·303 short magazine Lee-Enfield rifles between us! These were passed around, and we were given endless instructions on the mechanism and use of these weapons; far more deadly than my 4.10 shot gun, I secretly wished I could take one home to try out on our wild rabbit population. In due course, we all received a rifle, steel helmet, and gas mask.

One evening a week was to be deployed in drill and weapon training. Another time we would be out on 'manoeuvres' which entailed blacking our faces with Cherry Blossom boot polish, donning our steel helmets, and generally camouflaging ourselves with sprigs of laurel or beech, then four members of our platoon was sent ahead to reconnoitre. Our instructions being to "Approach and try to learn position, condition or strategic features of the 'enemy', without getting yourself discovered and shot." Led perhaps by Sergeant Rowles, we crawled along the bank of the River Lambourn, through high reeds, blackberry bushes and stinging nettles for the best part of one hour, doing our best to spot the other members of our platoon, who were acting as the 'enemy' up front. "Keep yer 'eads down you bloody fools, get us all shot." The order was hissed back down the line. On reaching our target marker, we quietly observe our imaginary opponents, made a few notes before retreating back to base. Plans were quickly drawn up by our 'superior'; calling up reserves we would attack at once, from two directions. We were greatly out-numbered but surprise and determination to defend our homeland gives us victory!

Of course, those imagined crack German Paratroopers quickly surrendered at the very sight of such an elite fighting force. Handing our prisoners over to the regular army, we then retired to take a well earned rest and celebrate victory over our pints at the Castle Pub!'

My service as a private in the Home Guard was not solely taken up in training. Other duties which would have proved beneficial in the event of invasion by paratroopers or saboteurs was to guard lonely desolate areas at night. We were allocated a four hour guard duty, quite tiring after a full day on the farm. There was in war time a vast uncultivated area above Red Farm, referred to as the Hidden Valley, it was no more than gravelly heathland covered with scrub bushes, gorse and in parts, dense undergrowth beneath a canopy of oak and conifer trees. Often cold and wet, the winds swept through the tall leafless trees on winter nights. An eerie landscape with the moon flitting between the racing clouds, casting weird shadows, one could easily imagine the devil himself lurking behind every tree or bush. Close by a dog fox howls to its mate, now a dark shadow as overhead an owl sets out on its nightly hunt for prey. A cock pheasant, unseen in some thick blackthorn, calls a warning to its harem of hens as human intruders disturb the quiet of the woods. The air-raid siren, perched on the top of Newbury Police Station, gives off its almost nightly long, loud bizarre wailing; warning everyone that enemy aircraft had crossed the English coastline and were now making their way inland to strike at some sleeping industrial town. Maybe tonight they wouldn't be carrying H.E. or incendiary bombs, it could be heavily armed troops instead.

Our instructions in the event of attack from the air was simple, no heroics, like intercepting the enemy single-handed. Hightail with all speed to inform our unit commander, we were there to give early warning, thus reducing the element of surprise. We had all done a course on how to spot and identify German aircraft. I knew for instance that the two engined Junkers JV88 with its single tail unit carried bombs beneath the centre section of the wings, whereas the Junkers JU90, a much larger aircraft, had a marked sweep-back on the low cantilever wing which carried its four engines in line abreast. The tail unit was of very large dimensions with twin fins and rudders. This plane was readily adaptable for use in the carrying and dropping of parachute troops. Tonight the planes were too high to identify, they droned on their way above the scattered cloud layer, making for the industrial midlands, search-light beams criss-crossed the night sky endlessly sweeping back and forth seeking out the intruders. The planes move on. There would be no parachutists dropping out of the sky tonight.

Looking back on those turbulent times, it is strange to recall that it wasn't the Germans I was afraid of. I was dead scared of my duty companion if the rota coupled me with Private Eli Cross. He was then in his 50's, the belligerent dairy farmer from Mousefield Farm. A great horseman, he was our units 'Cavalry Brigade', and always patrolled on horseback. Private Cross, well armed with a loaded shotgun, a mangle knife in his belt, plus two hand grenades, he had acquired dubiously from some unknown source, was the sort of man that would open fire and ask questions afterwards. Being almost stone deaf, if he challenged anyone in the dark, he could not have heard our password. I always made sure I knew of his whereabouts. It was amazing, he never shot any of our own men!

I wasn't on duty patrol the night of September 8th 1941, but it is certainly a night Sergeant Wilfred Rowles will not forget. At that time he was farming both Highwood and Red Farm. They already had two young daughters, Joan and Mary. An increase in the family was imminent, and in the early hours a high-speed dash to the maternity hospital in Reading had to be made despite the difficulties of driving in the blackout, shortage of petrol, and being flagged down on three or four occasions by over-enthusiastic home guard patrols, always wary of late night travellers as they manned make-shift road blocks. Swiftly explaining the urgency of his mission, he was waved on his way. Approaching the outskirts of our county town, the dark streets were deserted at that pre-dawn hour. It was now 3 am, not even the milkman had ventured out. Swinging into the hospital courtyard the old car shuddered to a halt at the main entrance, only just in time. Wilfred's wife Ethel gave birth to twin sons shortly afterwards, thus doubling his family overnight!

No doubt feeling pleasantly elated by the safe arrival of two sons, he was just having a quiet word with his wife when he was called to answer a telephone call of great urgency. "Blast it! Who the devil could that be, calling me here at this ungodly hour?" Snatching up the phone, he bellowed: "Yes, what is it?" "Sergeant Rowles? Brigadier Woods here, we've got a threat of invasion." Interrupting, Wilfred replied: "Threat of invasion, well its already taken place up here, we've had our own invasion tonight!" The irate military man cut him short: "This is serious Rowles, we have a "Red Alert", get back to your unit at once, call out all your men, full battle equipment, muster at battalion headquarters, await my further orders."

To save time, Wilfred phoned the Duty Sergeant, "Go to Red Farm, call out Corporal Toop, tell Donald to get his men together, tin helmets, rifles, the lot, get them all to Highwood." 'I'll be on my way at once!"

It was still pitch dark, Mum, Dad, my sister and I all fast asleep, peacefully unaware of Hitler's hostile intent. Bang, bang on the front door: "Whoever's that this time of the night?" I heard Dad say. Going downstairs in his dressing gown and slippers, he turns the key, door bolts slide back. "What's up?" He puts the question to the dim, uniformed figure on the doorstep. "Donald, Donald Toop here, get Bert up at once, and over to Brigade Headquarters at Donnington Priory, but first call in at Highwood. Wilfred and Sergeant Boswell should be there by now." Hearing this urgent conversation at the front door I had crept downstairs just in time to see the shadowy figure retreating down the garden path, at the gate he turned, shouted back, "Tell him, not to forget his tin hat, rifle and the ammo!" My Mother, who was up and fully awake by now, was in a rare old stew. "You 'alt to go as well, Frank." "No good me going" Dad replied. "What's the sense ole that? I got no gun or nothing. 'Sides, who's going to milk the cows in a bit?" Mum thought for a while before replying, "No good you milking them cows, nobody will want any milk with crowds of Germans running around the country." I had to admit that there was some logic in her words, but Dad had no intention of letting Hitler's army upset his farming routine!!

We had of course, been issued with arms, ammunition, and full kit by now. But whilst we had all taken our training seriously, it had really been only a game, now this was for real, and I must admit I was scared already, all the others would be there, I couldn't back out. Thousands of chaps a year or two older than me had seen action overseas, many to be killed, taken prisoner or wounded. Throwing on my oversize uniform, Mum fussed around. "Put your great coat on, Bert, it'll be cold outside."

I didn't stop to do up my black army issue boots, slinging my rifle over my shoulder, I got my bicycle out of the shed and off down our badly pot-holed gravel farm road. Daylight was just breaking in the east, low mist hung in our dry valley, sign of a bright, fine autumn day to come.

Our little group assembled at Highwood before marching over the hill to the Priory. On arrival in the courtyard, little groups of uniformed men stood around, no one seemed to know what was happening or what to expect next. Rumours were rife. The Germans had landed on the south coast in strength. A strong force had parachuted onto the Berkshire Downs near Aldworth. Heavily laden gliders were coming in over the Channel at this moment. It was broad daylight now, the early morning sun casting rays of sunshine through the great beech trees in the park, below which grazed a pedigree herd of Guernsey cows, oblivious to the commotion taking place on the other side of the fence.

Brigadier Woods and his superior, both looking very serious, now put in an appearance. "Right you men, form up immediately in battle order!" he barked. We had assembled many times before, and I would like to think we were reasonably well trained, some of course were First World War soldiers. Three abreast, some quick shuffling of army boots, dressing from left to right, we stood at attention. Sergeant Boswell about turned, stamped his feet, before giving a smart salute, which Brigadier Woods returned. "A smart turn-out" he barked in his best military manner. "You are all a credit to the community. However, I have to tell you that I'm afraid it has been a false alarm, no Germans have crossed our shores, and neither has there been confirmation of parachute drops. Nevertheless, tonight's exercise has been well worthwhile, and I have good reason to think that we are a well disciplined force to be reckoned with in the future if the need arose. I am proud of you all. Stand your men down, Sergeant!"

Such was action in the Home Guard. I suppose someone, some-where must have appreciated the sacrifice of so much time and effort

on our part. At the end of the War I was presented with a mahogany cigarette box adorned with a silver plaque and the words: "In gratitude from the people of Shaw-cum-Donnington". Inside was a crisp, new, one pound note!

My rifle, gas mask, great coat and uniform was handed back to the army stores. I kept my steel helmet which now resides, forgotten, in my gun cabinet, a nostalgic reminder of those turbulent years.

Service in the Royal Air Force

1941 drew to a close. The weather was grim, the news was grim, most of life's essentials were on ration, food was short, one waited patiently in queue for small luxuries. The war against Germany and her allies was going badly for England as we entered 1942, and it seemed only a matter of time before Hitler ordered his armies across the English Channel.

I was still working with my father on his small-holding, growing as much food as our meagre resources allowed. My old school friends had gone off to serve in the armed forces, some had already been killed, captured or wounded. Apart from my service in the Home Guard I didn't feel I was doing my bit. I was in a 'reserved occupation', but could volunteer for flying duties in the RAF or Fleet Air Arm. Not being a good sailor I chose the RAF, very much to my parents' disapproval. It was in the early months of 1942 that I joined the RAFVR (Royal Air Force Volunteer Reserve).

Directed to St. Giles' Hall, Reading for a medical examination I was passed A1; this was followed by three weeks of silence from the Air Ministry, I was beginning to think they had forgotten me, no doubt the feeling was that the war could still be won without my assistance. Then one morning the postman dropped a buff coloured envelope through the letterbox. I was instructed to appear at St. Peter's College Oxford, where I would sit an examination in English and Maths, in the meantime, I would get a short spell of tuition in both subjects three evenings a week by a retired head-master living in Ashmore Green. One month later I sat my examination and to my amazement passed with a reasonable grade. So much for the little country school in Love Lane and to my late Headmaster Mr Morris, he must have taught me something!!

On my sister's birthday, April 4th, the OHMS envelope arrived. News of my posting was a shattering blow to my parents. I was their mainstay for the farmwork, it was going to be a tough few years with me away and, whilst I was anxious to serve my country, I hated the thought of leaving them in the lurch.

Directed to report to St. John's Wood, London, a pass had been issued for my journey. Catching the 8.35 am train from Newbury Station on Monday, April 20th 1942. This steam locomotive must have left Penzance well before dawn.

Mum, Dad and Delcie saw me off, off to war, to do battle with the Germans, would I survive this conflict of great armies with modern weapons? I had had visions of being sent to an airfield in some quiet area, deep in the countryside, instead I was going to London, why

128

expose future aircrew to the dangers of almost nightly air-raids? It was beyond my comprehension. I had very mixed feelings as the train left the station. Leaning out of the carriage window, I gave my parents and only sister a last wave as we gathered speed, soon we were rushing through the fertile Thames Valley beyond Thatcham, with its lush green pastures. Next came Mr Goddard's well kept water meadows with his large herd of shorthorn milking cows. The fine stands of grain on the dead flat land of the Benyon Estate. I even caught a brief glimpse of the little white farmhouse at Beenham, my birthplace some twenty-one years earlier.

Was I doing the right thing? Should I have stayed home on the farm? I was very much a country yokel, teat pulling was the only trade I knew, I had serious doubts about my ability to fly a Wellington Bomber or a Spit-fire in a dog-fight with any great success. But the die was cast, I was going to fly with the RAF. There could be no turning back. In no time at all we were on the outskirts of Reading, passing to the rear of row upon row of tightly packed Victorian terrace houses, each with a brick built privy and wash house squeezed into a postage stamp size back-yard. It was a Monday morning, wash day, lines of newly washed clothes fluttered in the smoke laden atmosphere. How could anyone elect to live out their lives in such cramped conditions? Now and again a small white face peered from a tiny bedroom window. Some child yet too young to attend school, waved a frail, stick like arm at the passing train, I smiled, waved back, then we were gone. We stopped at Reading General. Carriage doors open, we lose some passengers gain some more. Mail, newspapers, parcels are unloaded. I lean out of the window, watching with interest this hive of activity, porters, travellers rush here and there, everyone seems to know where they are going, what they are doing. Inscrutable information is given out by the station announcer. The engine driver, leans out from his cab, coal blackened face partly hidden by the clouds of white steam rising from the engine's belly. Now carriage doors are slammed shut we are on our way again. The great express locomotive chuffs laboriously to move the long line of heavily laden coaches. Forty minutes later we pull into Paddington Station under the great domed glass roof, the end of the line.

London, the great metropolis, badly battered by aerial bombardment, but its people still defiant. I could count on one hand the number of times I had previously visited the City, now I would be stationed here. Stepping out onto the platform, clutching my small suitcase which contained my few possessions. Bowler hatted city types rushed past me, they knew just where they were going, their journey timed to the second. Soldiers, sailors, airmen, all in uniform, carried heavy kitbags, some going on leave, others returning. Two tall, powerfully built men in Airforce Blue uniforms, wearing red arm bands with MP in large black letters told all and sundry that they were military police. Any service man on the move could be stopped at any time and asked to produce his leave pass or travel voucher. Woe betide the man who couldn't produce the necessary documents.

I caught the number 74 bus to Lord's cricket ground, walking from there to St. John's Wood. I was surprised to see so little bomb damage in the area. I had expected to see vast sections of the city flattened.

My call-up papers gave 11 am as the time to report. It was now 10.30, at least I was in the right district. The buxom lady approaching looked a local person: "Can you direct me to Avenue Close Flats please?" "Yes, luv, up to the big cross roads, turn left, you will be in St. John's Wood Road; past Lord's cricket ground turn right into Grove End Road, the flats are just close by. You'll see some more lads around, its a new intake today. The previous flight went out the day before yesterday. I works there you see, in the cook-house, getting yer meals ready." "Thank you very much" I replied politely.

Striding on briskly carrying my suitcase and the small brown paper wrapped parcel which contained my favourite cake, date and walnut, plus some mincepies my Mother had made specially the night before. Avenue Close Flats stood back from the busy street, they had been luxury apartments before the War, now commandeered by the R.A.F. for training barracks. Forty-nine other raw recruits signed on that day, drawn from every corner of the British Isles, and a few from Britain's overseas possessions.

We were allocated rooms, I was to share a large bedroom with three other lads. Unpack, put everything away in the lockers provided, find your way to the canteen, where a meal would be served at thirteen hundred hours. The staff sergeant who had shown us to our rooms turned and vanished down a long corridor. "What's he mean thirteen hundred hours" I enquired of one of my new mates. "One o'clock, of course, you'll have to get used to twenty-four hour time keeping, its so's you don't get night-time muddled up with day-time, when we are told to go on guard duty or something, its what we will use on the planes too." "M'm, seems a bit daft to me, I always noos when it be night-time" was my reply.

I was soon to discover that life in the Air Force was going to be very, very different from the sheltered, peaceful, quiet existence I had led up to now on our Berkshire small-holding.

Lunch was to be followed by a lecture in the main hall. Sitting on rows of hard wooden charis an elderly high ranking officer gave us an extensive lecture, dwelling on the pride we must take in our new squadron, and in particular to uphold the fine traditions of the Royal Air Force. We would be allowed some free time. In the event of air raids, whilst not on duty we were to take cover in the nearest public air raid shelter, the underground stations could be used if the need arose. Finally we were warned of the danger of catching venereal disease if we associated with prostitutes. For me it was a very different way of life, new words, new dangers, all far removed from the soft green meadows of Dymond Farm, where the skylarks soar to meet the summer sun rising over Easton Copse, and the peewit swoops to distract the ploughman from her nest of eggs, or newly hatched chicks.

The first night was quiet, no enemy planes crossed the coasts at least there were no air raid sirens. We were up and about early, our corporal saw to that, opening bedroom doors and bawling "Wakey, wakey!" at the top of his voice. Day two was taken up with the issue of kit, more medicals, a dental inspection, various forms in triplicate to be completed – the long list of questions finished off with the name and address of next of kin, to be notified in the event of death or injury! Pessimistic lot these chaps.

The third day, 6.30 am, still only half awake, I could hear our corporal further down the corridor making his rounds. Now he opens our door "Wakey, wakey, rise and shine, on yer feet you horrible little men, I'm going to try and knock you lot into shape today." He moved on. Slowly we dragged ourselves free of army issue sheets and blankets covering a plain iron single bed. My new uniform of Air Force blue was a reasonable fit, but the material was coarse and the finish poor. It showed up badly against the American's uniforms when they entered the war a year or two later.

'Initial Training'. Square bashing we called it. Endless drills on our small parade ground. Route marches with full kit. Designed to 'knock us into shape' both mentally and physically. It wouldn't worry me, I was lean, tough and fit, years spent walking ploughed fields and country meadows had made me so. The other chaps, mostly townies would melt, they just weren't up to it. How desperately wrong I was. Parading and marching on hard ungiving tarmac was quite a different 'kettle of fish' from walking our fields at my own leisurely pace.

"Move!" bawled the drill corporal. "Come on, speed it up!" He sprinted to the rear of the gasping, panting column of fifty potential new aircrew, and urged us on from there. I was somewhere near the rear, jog-trotting laboriously with the rest, wondering how much longer I could keep going. My leg muscles protested, I tried to work out how many miles we had run. I had suspected nothing when we lined up outside our billets. We weren't clad in P.T. Kit, but in woollen pullovers and regulation slacks, and it seemed most unlikely that anything drastic was imminent.

The corporal, a cheerful little cockney, appeared to regard us with mild affection. He even had a pleasant smile. "Right lads, ten minutes rest, then we will make for the park." We needed no second telling, collapsing by the roadside. Talking amongst ourselves, someone said: "The park? does he mean Regents Park, we're miles from there, that's Parliament Hill on Hampstead Hill over there. The blighters brought us in the wrong direction." Groans of anguish greeted these words.

Our tormentor glanced at his watch, sprang to his feet, "Squad form up, we will march from here, and TRY (with heavy emphasis on the word), please try and keep in-step, we want to look like trained men, even if you're not!!"

This time he took the lead. "By the right quick march, eft-ight, eft-ight, eft-ight, eft-ight."

He set a cracking pace. It soon became apparent we were taking a different route back, much more tortuous than the outward journey. "Not much further now lads," shouted out the little corporal, trying to give some encouragement. We turned smartly into yet another street, iron railings and tall trees at the far end. Regents Park. I gritted my teeth, had I enough strength left to make it? I could see the entrance gate. Once inside we would get a rest, those that needed it a cigarette as well. I was getting cramp in my legs and sweating profusely. Gratefully we swung into the park, ready to flop down on the nearest patch of grass, but the corporal waived us on. "Come on lads, round the track." With that he broke into his jog-trot once more.

Reluctantly, we followed, occasionally he'd turn around, trotting backwards, allowing the line of panting recruits to pass him. This time he'd bring up the rear using obscene language on the stragglers. The circuit was completed. "Right, fall out." he commanded. "Thank God for that." I thought, collapsing on the grass with the rest of my exhausted mates. It seemed but a few minutes before "On yer feet lads, we are going round again." We stared at him in disbelief, a storm of protest broke out. "Aw, no corp, have a heart." The smile vanished from our corporal's face. "You chaps think I'm being tough." He retorted. "Wait till you get to ITW, its worse there than in the guards, I'm just breaking you lot in gently, you'll thank me for it later. Right, at the double, this time, one-two, one-two, one-two, one-two, faster, faster. Fatigue duty tomorrow for anyone that drops out!"

Back at the canteen, I just managed to shuffle along with the rest, clutching my mug and plate to receive my ration of cocoa, sausage, beans and a slice of buttered bread. We had a flight lecture in the afternoon. I wasn't the only one to fall asleep!!

Early morning drill on the parade ground followed by lectures, maths and navigation filled our days. We all took our turn on guard duty at the RAF HQ, Viceroy Court. Our uniform, spotless, black boots highly polished, brass buttons burnished, belts and cap flashes brilliant white. A never ending stream of foreign dignitaries, members of parliament and commission officers, with rank high enough to have 'scrambled egg' on the peak of their cap passed continuously through the large mahogany door.

I spent some months in London during the Blitz, my mates and I had many adventures, some good, some bad. Our time was mainly occupied by learning navigation and the morse code. Simulated flight experience was gained in Link Trainers.

I made two close friends in the Squadron. Limited off duty hours found us travelling on the underground to the West End. With luck we sometimes escorted a WAAF apiece to some pub for a drink or a visit to the 'Windmill'. Our first period of aircrew training was completed. We finished leaner, tougher and with a smattering of knowledge in the theory of flight. Soon we would be moving on.

Life Under Canvas

"Our postings are through, we are on the move". The news spread like wild fire. "Where are we going to?" the question was voiced time and again. Someone said we were moving to East Anglia, another knew for sure we were being transferred to Scotland. He'd heard the news on sound authority. Some flights had even gone to Canada to complete their training. A posting overseas had not been ruled out. It was certain to be on some nice airfield tucked away in a quiet part of the country, so that we could continue our flight training in peace, away from wartime London with its battered streets and buildings, air raids, and the detonation of shells from the ack-ack guns.

Finally, when we did get confirmation, our destination proved a non-event. A damp, watermeadow on the bank of the little river Teme just out of Ludlow in Shropshire. We were sure it was simply a last dash of spite, our untiring little corporal had us all out of bed by 5 am to catch the 11 am from Paddington Station. Kit bags had to be packed, our rooms left spotless, bedding folded in the approved manner. Breakfast over, we marched to the station. A special train had been laid on which was to take us through Reading, Oxford, and Hereford, finally arriving at Ludlow Station at 16.30 hours. Met at the station by a staff sergeant and two corporals, we mustered in the roadway watched by a small knot of curious school children. It seemed that airmen were an unusual sight in this quiet back-water.

We marched with full kit to our new camp. The rain fell in unremitting sheets blown by a strong southwesterly. To say we were wet was the understatement of the year. Some three miles out of town we turn off the B4361 into a waterlogged meadow. A row of green camouflaged tents stood in line by the river bank. One could think of untold beautiful camp sites in the British Isles, yet some desk-bound idiot had to choose this one. Close to a large oak tree, two men worked under a makeshift canvas shelter. This was the cook-house. They had prepared hot soup, vegetable stew with a small cube of meat if you were lucky, this made us a very welcome supper, even though we had to stand to eat, or sit on wet kit-bags.

Its a tight squeeze, eight men in one small bell-tent with all your belongings, there is not much room for privacy! The rain continued all night, our tent leaked, water ran in one side and out the other, we could have kept just as dry outside! Next day at the first opportunity we dug a shallow trench all around the outside of our tent, hopefully this would run most of any further rainwater away.

One advantage of being under canvas, if one came back late after an evening visit to the local town, it was possible to creep into the tent from the rear after dark, but that hardly compensates for the luxury of our accommodation in London with real beds, and clean sheets. Trying to sleep on duck boards is not to be recommended, but at least there were no air-raids!

Next day, I decided to tackle our quarter-master, pleading for a tent that didn't leak, pointing out to him, that should eight potential fighter pilots succumb to pneumonia, it wouldn't help the war effort one little bit. Two days later we got a new tent. We managed to acquire a large number of used bricks with which we laid a firm, dry pathway, this made for far less mud being taken into the interior of our tent. Being useful at carpentry, I made a wooden construction to hang our plates, mugs and Wellington boots on.

Slowly the camp became more organised, Morse, maths and navigation classes began once more. This was the first time any section of the RAF had been stationed in this area: June 4th 1942 my notes tell me I had my first shave since May 27, kneeling on a rock at the river edge, and using the clear cool waters as a mirror!

We had discarded our uniforms for the time being, and were now kitted out with battle dress.

There was little to occupy our time during off duty periods and war-time Ludlow offered precious little in the way of night life. Going into town one afternoon my mate Dennis and I hired a boat and rowed down the river Theme. In places it is dangerous with fast currents. Ignoring danger signs we came too close to the weir and were almost swept over, we were completely done in after our struggle to get clear. In off duty hours I worked for a Mr Davies hand-planting potatoes for one shilling per hour. When he found out I could drive, he had me driving his old Standard Fordson. Ridging for potatoes, chain harrow and muck cart.

There was no church parade on Sundays out in the sticks, and most of the local people attended chapel. We soon found that by joining the congregation we got invited back to their home for lunch, even had our washing done for us. They were kind, generous people, but any daughters were well chaperoned.

June 23rd 1942. A week's leave is granted, my first. I caught the 12.12 pm from Ludlow station to Shrewsbury. Stopping at every station plus a few more not marked on the map, it is a very slow journey. Having changed trains once, it was 5.40 before we pulled into Oxford Station. Rather than go on to Reading, I started to walk the twenty-eight miles home. As things turned out I did the journey in three hours, thumbing lifts in five different vehicles!

June 29 1942. Our squadron, fitter, hardier, after a summer out at grass, was posted to No 13 ITW Torquay. June 30 we muster on our now dry parade ground, and march with full kit, in step now, and with arms swinging up to the shoulder of the man in front, hands clenched with thumbs pointing forward. Proudly through the town where we had made good friends with the locals in our short stay. At the rail head, a two coach troop-train waited, the engine with full steam up was to take its light load of airmen non-stop through the stations of Hereford, Abergavenny, Pontypool, Caerleon, here the line swings in a wide loop at Newport before turning east to run alongside the river Severn until we vanished into the tunnel which gives a short cut to Bristol. A short stop here, but we were not allowed off the train. Restocked with coal and water, with a fresh crew we were away on the last lap of our journey. Taunton next, now steaming south-west through picturesque Devon, briefly I thought how sad it would be to have a foreign power rule and control this beautiful land of ours.

We stop outside Exeter before getting an all clear signal; we have swung south now as the line runs on the very edge of the wide mouth of the river Exe, now along the coast to Dawlish, Teignmouth, then inland once more, Newton Abbott and finally draw into Torquay station at 7 pm; dirty, tired and very hungry.

We are to take a ten week course at Torquay, working mostly from the Grand Hotel which has been commandeered by the RAF. Included in our daily activities was long distance route marching, rock climbing, an assault course, tuition in unarmed combat and instructions in the event of chemical warfare for which we are issued with gas mask and special clothing.

Dinghy practice: I can think of more suitable clothing for a swim in the warm sea water of Torbay, a much more enjoyable method than the one thought up by our PT instructor. Dressed in full battle dress we jumped, if not voluntarily, then with some physical persuasion from the drill sergeant off the end of the pier, a twenty foot drop. There was no fear of drowning in the choppy seas, as we were kitted out with mae-wests. We now struck out ponderously making for inflated bomber dinghies, somehow we dragged ourselves aboard then waited patiently to be rescued by motor launch.

I just hoped I didn't have to do this exercise for real!

After ten weeks slog we take our exams in maths, navigation and meteorology spread over two days. It was more than a week later that we heard the result. D Flight number 2 Squadron posed for a photo in full flying kit.

A celebration party was planned, just a small get together with a few eats and plenty of beer. Unfortunately my mate Phil and I got caught in the open whilst making our way there. The air raid warning sounded and almost immediately eight Foche-Wulfe 190's swept in just above the waves. Flying at about five hundred feet they had come in below the radar screen. These planes, fighter bombers, carried a five hundred lb. bomb slung below the fuselage and upon release become a formidable fighter plane. I had learnt from previous experience that if a bomb is released with the plane directly above you its not you that should be worried, but if you see it released, as we did on this occasion, whilst the plane is some 500 to a 1000 yards in front, watch out! As heavy machine gun bullets cut up the ground we dived for the cover of a brick wall. Almost immediately the bomb exploded, some 30 or 40 yards away, completely demolishing many houses. Phil and I were flung some distance into the middle of the street. I had a knee injury from a piece of shrapnel but apart from shock we were both in one piece.

We never did get to our party. Phil and I set to helping the local defence and ARP personnel dig out dead and injured survivors. I well remember hearing cries for help coming from a badly damaged house, following the call to an upstairs bedroom, I found an elderly lady, covered in dust and pinned by part of the roof which had collapsed, trapping her against the wall. Using a long piece of timber as a lever, Phil and I managed to get her free. "Thank you, thank you; please find my money its in the bed. My money, my money!" Despite the fact that the roof of her house had been blown off, the only things she seemed to worry about was her money. Sure enough we found this small biscuit tin. Once she had that her life seemed to return to normal.

Torquay was badly damaged in this short, sharp hit-and-run raid, the Germans were conducting a series of this type of attack around our shores.

My uniform which had been torn and damaged was cleaned and repaired. I thought I might have got a new one but no such luck. At this time we were issued with full flying kit. All in one fur-lined jacket, three pairs of gloves, sheep wool lined boots, and full length white socks. (In later years these same socks came to light every Christmas Eve to hang at the foot on my childrens' bed awaiting the annual visit of Father Christmas.)

At long last we were moved to an RAF air field further inland and were surrounded by real planes even though they were only trainers – far more exciting than poring over maps plotting imaginary flights across Europe.

Before leaving Torquay, two of my mates, Phil, Ken and myself, did manage to get into a celebration dinner. This was at the Drum Hotel, Cockington. It was mutually agreed that now we had been promoted to L.A.C.'s (Leading Aircraftmen) and our pay increased to five shillings and sixpence per day. Just this once two shillings each spent on a slap-up meal would not go amiss, after all it's pointless saving your money in wartime, we all agreed!

From my wartime diary my notes state that I first flew in a Tiger Moth on September 10th, airborne at 10.16 hours, up and away into a cloudless autumn morning. Flying for 40 minutes before my Rhodesian instructor took over the dual controls to land smoothly in the gentlest of touch-downs on the grass runway. On the 11th, we took off for 59 minutes, and so the summer passed, and with winter's approach there was less good flying weather.

Ill health was to bar me from operational flying. In the latter days of the war I was posted with the survivors of our squadron to Blackpool. At the RAF headquarters Rex Hallet and I were given an address where we were to be billetted for the time being: Mrs Connley, 229 Central Drive, Blackpool. On arriving there she kindly gave us a meal, all the time chatting away in her strong Lancashire accent, which I found most difficult to understand.

Years have slipped by, often I have wondered about the fortunes of my wartime colleagues in No. 2 Squadron, how many of those bright, eager young men survived the conflict. Very, very few I imagine. It would have been interesting to have kept in touch, but I never did.

Before returning to civvy street with bands playing, much pomp and ceremony on the parade ground, myself and quite a few others were decorated by the Under Secretary of State. By command of the Air Council.

Finally, decked out in an ill-fitting, coarse cloth herring-bone demob suit, with my tin medal in its little box tucked away in a pocket, my few belongings stuffed into my much travelled suitcase, a free rail-pass got me back to Newbury Station once more.

In due course, like the rest of the ex-servicemen, the State gave me a small gratuity, hardly enough to set me up in a farm of my own, but nevertheless most welcome.

Thus ended the Second World War, and I returned to the only job I really knew! Farming.

Some Interest in a Land Army Girl

Home from the war. To my father's relief I set to working alongside him on his small holding, Dymond Farm.

Life on the farm was very much the same except that now we had a Fordson Tractor and milked a few extra cows. My mother's cooking was as good as ever, only now I really did appreciate her culinary arts. It was as though all the long years of war, such dreadful, mindless destruction with millions dead, or maimed for life, was just a bad dream. Unfortunately, for so many life would never be the same again. The English countryside including our own small patch looked just the same as before I went away, apart from the fact that now there was much more land under the plough.

On my return to civvy life, one of the first jobs I did was to service 'Teddy' our Fordson tractor, fill up with TVO hitch on the two furrow ransome trailer plough and head for Big Easton. A thirteen acre, neglected poultry farm which I had purchased early in the war years from a Mr Wilkins, who had retired from egg production. His asking price of one thousand pounds was eventually whittled down to six hundred and fifty pounds, £50 per acre.

My father considered it was far too high a price to pay for such poor gravel, sandy soil. First I marked out the headland, turning over a single shallow furrow five or six yards from the outside of the field. This strip was for turning at the end of each bout and would be turned over last. Then with three flag sticks placed in line across the field twenty yards out from the headland mark, I turn the first furrows over, turn around and back across the field again. I marked out the whole field, quite a lengthy process, a tedious job, todays ploughmen don't have to. They work with the modern reversible hydraulic ploughs. Whilst ploughing a field one should keep ones eye very much on the work in hand if you wish to do a good job and strike a straight furrow, but I couldn't fail to notice a uniformed land-girl working down a long line of six by four poultry houses in the adjoining field.

On reaching the end of the turn, when but fifty yards and a boundary hedge separated us, I gave a lighthearted wave, she looked across, but there was no return wave, no response whatever. I tried again on the next turn, but still no acknowledgement, just a stoney stare. "Ah well, I'm not one to give up easily, something will turn up one day. I just had a keen desire to speak to the lass, somehow, somewhen.

The opportunity didn't arise until mid-summer of the same year. A phone call to my father from our neighbour, Keith Simpson, "I've got about fifteen acres of good mowing grass around the poultry pens, would you care to send your son over, and cut them for hay? If you make a good job of cutting and clearing you can have the grass free." Isn't it strange how fate can take a hand, and change one's whole life like a sudden switch of the wind, this time just on a telephone call?

"Would you like to go over to ole Simpson's place, cut the grass in the poultry paddocks, he's given us the crop, make a bit of extra hay for the Winter, could come in very useful." said Dad. "OK" I replied, trying not to show too much enthusiasm. I spent an hour cleaning up our old Fordson, then turned my attention to the Bamford mower. It was our old original horse drawn mower, the long pole having been sawn off and a tractor hitch fitted. It still boasted the iron seat, and on occasions, if we were cutting a heavy crop or the wind was troublesome, Dad would drive the tractor and I would sit on the mower seat, and drag back the grass with a fork or hay rake, as it fell before the blade.

With a light heart, I set off for the next farm. "Would I see her again, and if so what were the chances of getting into conversation?" It would take up to a week, to cut, turn, make and cart fifteen acres of hay especially if it was in many small paddocks. During the day, this land girl spent a lot of time out of sight working in the incubator building, but came out late afternoon to feed some of the growing pullets. On the excuse of walking back home with a five gallon can to get some more T.V.O., I made sure I would pass where she was working. "Hello" I said, rather weakly, "I've been waving to you for the last six months without a reply". "I know, I've seen you" she replied. "But there are six men working on this farm, plus a fat batchelor farmer, and they have all tried to get fresh at some stage over the four years I've been working here on this so and so poultry farm. I'm waiting for my boy-friend to return from a German prisoner of war camp. I don't wish to give any encouragement to a tractor driver. Now if you don't mind, I've got work to do, even if you haven't. I wasn't getting far, it seemed a blank wall. Why was it that all the nicest, prettiest girls I had ever met were already spoken for? Surely, I won't always be second best?

It took me two days to cut the fifteen acres in the time available between milkings. Many stops were necessary to resharpen the mower knife. The grass in poultry pens doesn't get harrowed and rolled, and not being grazed with livestock can be tough in the bottom. The ground is rough and uneven, caused by the laying birds constantly scratching small hollows to dust themselves. The farm looked tidier already, but the hay would be dry, dusty, and with little feed value, but this didn't concern me too much. The main thought in my mind was that I had a genuine excuse for being on Simpson's poultry farm, and I was determined to strike up another conversation with the land army girl whom I had discovered was called Peggy Day, and lived in digs in Thatcham, travelling back and forth each day on a bicycle.

The weather held fine and dry with just enough wind from the South West to make perfect hay. On small meadows, we still turned cut grass with wooden hand rakes. A laborious task usually performed by the whole family. "There will be no need for you, to come over to Simpson's place to turn the hay," I told my father. I can get some help from the poultry workers in the evening. My plan was to spend as long as possible turning those few almost worthless, weedy acres. If we were to avoid dead, or at the very least some sick cows next Winter, I would also have to collect up all the ragwort and burn it!

This well run poultry farm was an accredited breeding unit turning out sexed day olds, and growing pullets which were despatched daily to all parts of the British Isles. The breeding stock. Four or five hundred pure bred Rhode Island or Light Sussex hens were free range in two acre paddocks with fifteen to twenty mature cockerels for company. Housed in well-ventilated, long wooden purpose built houses, one to each section. Foxes were a problem. To protect the stock, the whole farm was surrounded by a fox proof fence. Six feet high, the strong diamond shaped galvanised fence was capped by an outward sloping defence of three strands of deadly barbed wire. The mesh wire was dug into the ground twelve inches to prevent foxes digging beneath. But with all this defence crafty reynard still managed to get the occasional dinner. A tree branch broke the fence on a rough night or someone left a gate open. This meant the hens had to be shut up at night. The staff took turns to do this job, which, with 'double' summertime could mean eleven o'clock, before the day's work was finished.

Each of the workers did a week's tour of duty on 'nights', with this arrangement their stint came round every six weeks or so. I made discreet enquiries through Luke, one of the more talkative farmworkers, only to learn with disappointment that the land-girl had done her turn at shutting up two weeks previous, so no way would her next tour of duty clash with haymaking, unless we had a months wet weather!!!

Once more fate was to take a hand, the wife of one of the men had gone into labour four weeks early. The girl took his place. The next day I found an excuse to have a word with Simpson: "Had I cut all the grass to his satisfaction? I will be turning the hay that afternoon and evening, do you mind if I help your girl to shut up the hens later on? Replying in his gruff voice, he said: "Huh, like that is it? Got yer eye on that young Peggy Day 'ave you?" "Your father sent you over here to make hay not make off with my female staff! Well, I can't stop you I suppose, but no hanky-panky round the poultry houses, and don't keep her out too late, she's got to be here at 7.30 sharp every morning."

The weather held, a light, south-west wind, soon made this rather old grass mellow in the sun. I turned each swathe with my antiquated wooden rake, working well into the evening as the sun set in the west. She was doing her rounds, working through the unit towards the paddock I was working in. If one waited until it was pitch dark, the hens would go to roost. But in the half light of dusk, one old hen would decide to sit at the trap-door entrance, preventing the rest from going up the little slatted ramp. Since there was such a lot of hen houses to shut, one tried to drive the birds in early, and thus get the job finished. Has the reader ever tried driving hens? They are the most stupid livestock on the farm, although they go up and down those ramps a dozen times each day, at dusk they just hop past and round the corner of the hen house, deliberately missing the wide open trap-door.

Now in my paddock where I was still turning hay in an absent-minded fashion, she started driving the hens to roost. It was a warm summer's evening, she was clad in khaki shorts, and not wearing much up top. I couldn't help but notice her suntanned limbs and slim figure. She meant business with those hens, and moved with determination, even so they didn't intend going to roost before dark, if it could be avoided. "Do you want some help, I enquired? If I went round the other way, we might get somewhere." "Yes, you may as well, you aren't doing any good leaning on that rake!"

With two of us, we soon had those hens tucked up for the night, but it was now 10.30 pm, and quite dark. She had to cycle five or six miles back to her lodgings with the Browns in Northfield Road, Thatcham. Have supper and be back at work next morning by 7.30 am. Six days a week, for £2-5-0, plus one shilling and three pence (old money) per hour overtime pay. I volunteered to see her to the main road: "Can't take you home, I haven't a bicycle." "There's no need, thank you. I've been making the journey on my own quite safely for the last four years."

I was enjoying life, haymaking by day, and shutting up old Simpson's hens in the evening. Come Thursday there was an extra chore to be done. She had to turn the eggs in the incubator building. This hatchery had upwards of ten thousand eggs down at any one time. The day-old chicks were sexed, and sent all over the British Isles, mainly in small cardboard boxes by rail. There was a ready market for the pullets but most of the cockerels would be gassed and then sold as meat to a local mink breeding farm.

Peggy was definitely 'thawing' out, she was not so hostile to me, and we never seemed to run out of conversation, we had been on speaking terms, so to speak, for four days. Tonight we worked silently turning the hatching eggs, the building was dimly lit by low voltage electric bulbs. After an hour or so, the last tray was slid back into position, quietly, I held her hand in mine, and before she quite knew what to expect, I kissed her. Surprisingly, she didn't protest.

From then on our friendship never looked back, growing from strength to strength, and we were never happier than when in each other's company.

My Courtship of Peggy Day

Peggy Olive Day. Land Army Girl. Pretty, shapely, vivacious, well educated, only child of Mr F.H. Day, Chief Cashier at a London Bank, and his wife, Olive. They lived at No. 10 Birch Avenue, Tilehurst, on the outskirts of Reading, Berkshire. Mr Day, who had survived the First World War, had high hopes for his bright daughter. Educated at the John Radcliffe School, she had taken and successfully passed, a course in shorthand typing. This was to be her career with the Prudential Insurance Company. At the outbreak of the Second World War, with the young men being called up for the colours, women were required in jobs more essential than typing. Not wishing to go into a munition factory, nor join the armed forces, Miss Day and her cousin, Betty Tribe, decided that the Women's Land Army, working and caring for animals in the beautiful English countryside, was to be their War effort.

I firmly believe that some Higher Deity maps our short span on earth well in advance. Miss Day's decision to work on the land was to lead to a lifetime on the farm, and the busy, demanding role of a farmer's wife. Much to the initial dismay of Mr & Mrs Day, who certainly didn't agree with their daughter's choice. They had been looking forward to the end of the war and their daughter's return to a more civilised way of life, the clean, paved streets, a nine to five job, five days a week, with chapel on Sundays. That nice young man, George Wyatt would soon be home from prison camp in Germany. Instead she chose to spend her life on a farm. Somewhere in the depth of the Berkshire countryside where county bumpkins worked seven days a week, three hundred and sixty-five days a year, seldom looking at the clock. The monetary returns for all this hard labour was minimal. The wellie boot is a must, but worse of all, to a city dweller, is the repugnant farmyard smells, not to mention the swarms of flies in the summertime.

But there, I'm jumping the gun, you've got the last chapter first! I've spoilt the story!

The last trapdoor was closed, the last reluctant hen now gone to roost. Old farmer Simpson fast asleep.

"Can I see you home tonight?" I asked of my new attraction. "I'll soon run across the fields, collect my bike and meet you at the bottom of the farm road." "If you wish, but I do know the way home, you know!" she replied. "Well, maybe you think you do, but I'll show you a short cut to Thatcham."

Back at our farmhouse, I'm getting my cycle out of the shed. In my rush I knock down some of Dad's tools, which were always stacked in their correct places. "Where ever are you going to at this time of night?" my mother enquired of me. "The land girl on ole Simpson's farm has been helping me turn the hay, so I'm going to see her safely back to her lodgings in Thatcham," I replied. "I've noticed you have been very late back from hay-making those last few nights, who is this land girl and where does she come from, you don't know anything about her, do you?" "OK Mum, don't you go worrying about me, I've been in the Air Force, been around a bit, and I am twenty-four in case you've forgotten."

"Well behave yourself, don't go getting serious. There are plenty of nice farmer's daughters around, most would make a much better wife than some unknown land girl." "Don't be daft Mum, who said anything about getting married, I'm only seeing the girl home!" It was nearly always my mother who gave her opinion on family matters. Dad was easy going, letting the world go by, he never worried about anything.

Despite this parental caution, I continued to court Peggy Day during the following summer months. I showed her the short cut through Easton Copse, and over the stile to Stoney Lane. Follow this road to Ashmore Green and one could quickly get to Thatcham. Just depending how long we dawdled in the leafy shade of a certain giant oak tree!

The hay at Simpson's farm was eventually carted home loose on our tractor trailer, stacked in the barn for winter fodder. Peggy and I were now great friends. Most evenings after work on the poultry farm was done, she came to help with our haymaking. Working together we turn the thick swathes of hay with wooden rakes. She helped with the carting and building of ricks, a long arduous task, but the sun seemed to shine for days on end during that lovely summer, and with the whole family, and some village helpers, it was happy, pleasant work, with tea and a slice of cake in the shade of a

partly made rick. The sweet smell of mellow, well made meadow
hay. Its just something special and unforgettable, but those days have
gone. Today, the tractor driver with his round baler doing the work
of a dozen men, has only his radio/cassette player for company.

My mother, with her strict Victorian upbringing, didn't approve of
my new friend's very short shorts, thin cotton shirt, and no bra. She
voiced her opinion in no uncertain terms. From my point of view, I
approved, I found it most attractive, certainly the lack of clothes
showed off Peggy's young bronze-coloured limbs to perfection. The
corn harvest followed, cutting the wheat with the binder, stooking
the sheaves, then after the stooked corn had heard the church bells
ring on three consecutive Sundays it was loaded with pitchforks onto
horse drawn wagons, and carted to the rick-yard, where my father
built immaculate well shaped ricks.

Work didn't occupy all our time. Peggy and I went for long cycle
rides, exploring country lanes that even I had never travelled on,
occasionally getting lost down some narrow overgrown cart track
that led to nowhere!

147

I plucked up courage, took her to visit my Grandparents who farmed at Hoe Benham, something one didn't do unless one was 'going steady'! It was with some surprise that I got an invitation to visit her parents at Tilehurst. It appeared they wished to meet the young man their daughter was spending so much time with!

I went to tea one Sunday. It was a bit nerve racking, but I felt I was well received and I really fell for Peggy's mother. She was a very pleasant, happy person, making me feel very much at home, and one of the family. Mr Day occasionally fired questions at me. Mainly concerning farm life, what stock we kept, how many cows we milked, did we have pigs, do we have time to go to Church or Chapel on Sundays? I thought he was very green on matters of the countryside, but then he was a city business man, I was an ambitious young farmer with eyes on his only daughter. We were worlds apart.

I had already taken on the tenancy of Mousefield Farm. Sixty-eight and a half acres, the house and all the buildings for a rent of £150 per annum. Col. Walker, the landlord had let the house off separately, and it didn't become vacant until the Spring of 1946. The house was in a shocking condition, the kitchen floor had rotted away, the walls were damp, and covered in green mildew, rats and mice scurried around in the roof and in the store cupboards, the lovely old vegetable garden was six feet high with weeds, and the surrounding quick thorn hedge hadn't been cut for ten years or more.

With secret plans in my mind, I took Peggy to see the now empty farmhouse, and it was on the doorstep, under the little red porch with ivy covered trestle-work sides that I asked her to marry me. Her answer surprised me. "You've been a long time thinking about it, I thought you were never going to pluck up enough courage to ask me!" Kissing me full on the lips, she then said: "Of course, I will, I do love you, you know, I fell for my farmer in the hay-field last Summer, but we can never live here in the state this house is in, Mummy will have a fit when she sees it!"

Mousefield Refurbished

Peggy Day, loyal member of the Women's Land Army, had accepted my proposal of marriage. From that day forth, life took on a more urgent meaning, there was so much preparation in hand, so much planning for the future. We both worked with renewed vigour every spare evening, and at weekends if farm tasks allowed. Mousefield Farmhouse has great character, sadly it had been neglected for so long. Because we were happy together, it seemed to be a happy house, a family home, one could imagine fun and laughter vibrating from the centuries old oak beams.

Both sets of parents seemed delighted with the match, wishing us well. They all joined in with the cleaning, scrubbing, removing the accumulation of dust and cobwebs, painting, repairing doors and windows. I caught the rats and mice by every means possible, obtained two good tabby cats which were turned loose in the barn. Cut the overgrown garden hedge, slashed down the rampant weeds. In a short time our future home was transformed.

We would need furniture, lots of it, but new was on ration, and could not be purchased unless a young couple gave the date of their marriage. I sent off the necessary form, carefully answering all the questions. Yes, I was British, had served in the Armed Forces, had no other furniture, stated my age, and that we were to be married on September 28th. I cannot remember if they wished to know the colour of my eyes, but there was precious little they didn't know about us by the time I got to the bottom of the form, and had signed it!

In due course we were issued with dockets, sufficient to allow the purchase of a kitchen table and four chairs, or a double bed, wardrobe and chest of drawers. It was mutually decided that there was little point in getting married if we didn't have a double bed. The vote came out in favour of spending our precious dockets on a bedroom suite. This 'utility' furniture as it was called served us well in the following years, and it's still in use in the twin bedroom in 1987!

I have always been able to turn my hand to woodwork. From an old barn door I made a kitchen table, we sat on two 'thirty dozen' egg boxes stood on end until eventually I fashioned two three-legged stools.

In anticipation of our forthcoming marriage I would have to hunt around for some second-hand furniture, but it was expensive and hard to come by. One day in town, I bumped into my Uncle, Douglas Houghton. He was a builder, specialising in the restoration of old or run down properties. He mentioned in conversation that he had purchased a house in Great Bedwyn, complete with all its contents, the owners having returned to the United States. "I hear you are getting married shortly, come and have a look, I'll sell you a house full of furniture."

Come Saturday morning we were both full of excitement, could we afford to purchase a house-full of furniture and effects anyway? Uncle Doug drew up at the farm-gate in his thirty hundred weight builders truck, it was a tight squeeze with the three of us in the front seat. We sped along the A4, meeting little traffic on the journey. Just before Savernake Forest, we turned off to our left and soon arrived at our destination.

Stopping at a quaint thatched cottage in the centre of the village. My uncle opened the small front gate and led the way through the neat little garden to a porch over-hung with clematis. Unlocking the door, he led the way inside. Peggy and I looked at each other, we were both speechless. The cottage was a treasure house, every room upstairs and down was packed with antique and period furniture!

In particular I admired the beautifully polished oval mahogany dining table, surrounded by twelve George III Chippendale style leather-seated chairs.

The floors both downstairs and up, were covered in the best Wilton or Axminster carpets; a superb mahogany sideboard with a delightful over-mantle caught my eye. In the kitchen was an oak breakfast table and six matching 19th Century chairs. A pretty suite in the lounge appeared to have been recently recovered. There were eastern rugs, Chinese porcelain, old horse brasses, brass candlesticks, pewter mugs, pictures on the walls and bric-a-brac on every available shelf and window sill.

The little cottage garden had been well maintained: "What about the two garden seats, Uncle Doug?" "Oh yes, they are included, also the lawn mower and lots of tools," he replied. "You've bought everything here then, Uncle" I said. "Yes, the house and all the contents, lock, stock and barrel; I'm only interested in the property, I thought all this stuff here would just set you two up, good quality antique furniture will always hold its value, these people paid a lot of money for all this before the War. If you clear it all away in the next day or two, and leave the place tidy, you can have the lot for £300. I know I could make a lot more money if I sold it off in bits and pieces, but I want it all gone quick and in one lot. I've got a good customer lined up for this place, so I want to get my men in for a few days, square a few jobs up, then get it sold, I can't afford to have the money tied up for long."

"It's just what I could do with Uncle Doug, but I haven't got the sort of money you're asking. Tell you what I'll do though. Move everything right away and give you two hundred pounds in cash. It will be all profit after you sell the house." He smiled and said. "You're a tight'un, no mistake. If I let you have all this lot for that money, don't expect a Wedding Present!"

I gave him two hundred one pound notes on our return to the farm. He loaned me the key. It took Peggy and I four days to clear our purchase. We could only make one trip per day with tractor and farm trailer. The standard Fordson now on rubber wheels is not the fastest tractor on the road. Peggy sat on a bale of straw in the trailer on the outward journey, but on the return trip she had to sit side-saddle on the tin mud-guard whilst I bounced up and down on the iron seat!

We could only park in the village street, so everything had to be carried down the garden path. It was hard, demanding work, but we were blissfully happy, like two birds building a nest in spring.

Chairs were stacked on tables, bedding, rugs, and carpets on top, breakables carefully wrapped up in old newspapers then placed in tea chests and boxes. Sorting through cupboards or hidden in corners we found many more treasures.

Tied down with ropes the whole assortment looked like a travelling junk shop, we must have looked like two Romany Gypsies on the move! Except of course, they would have used horse drawn transport.

Back at the farm our conglomeration was unloaded and piled on the lawn. It was great fun setting it all in place. The old farmhouse

took on a new look once more, with carpets on the floor, curtains hung and furniture installed.

The house at Mousefield has stood on the same site for centuries, much altered and changed with succeeding generations no doubt, but always a great family home. Once more it was destined to become the home of a new farming family. It seemed pleased with its new occupants.

With its unique character and sheltered position it stands majestically surrounded by its attendant cluster of farm buildings in red brick and tile. The huge 17th century barn, built of course for a different era in farming history, is unusual in its architectural design. There were very few constructed with an 'eye-brow' roof covering the great oak doors.

Looking out across the dry valley officially designated an area of outstanding natural beauty. We overlook the market town of Newbury set in a basin some two miles distance to a range of chalk hills on the horizon which includes Beacon Hill, Heaven's Gate and Inkpen Beacon.

Above our house to the north-east we are sheltered by twenty-acres of ancient coppiced woodland with a great stand of mature oaks, silver birch and ash. Our wood is beautiful at any time of the year, but especially so in the Spring, the trees coming into leaf and the floor beneath covered with primroses, wood anemones and its dense carpet of bluebells. We get the dawn chorus of the many bird species through the open bedroom window, foxes, squirrels, badgers and the deer are all active after the hard winter months.

In recent years our nature trails are open to the public on certain days, this is really just to share the beauty with others, not so fortunate as ourselves.

Wedding Bells

Having asked Mr Day for his daughter's hand in marriage in the traditional manner, Peggy and I fixed the date of our wedding for September 28th 1946. It would have to be after the harvest was safely gathered.

In the event, harvest that year was a late one, and it turned out to be a close run race. The last sheaves of corn were pitched to the top of the last rick on the evening of the 27th. Fourteen hours to go before I was due at 2.30 pm to take my place in the front pew of Oxford Road Methodist Church, Reading, to await my intended bride on her father's arm. My first cousin, Jack Perris had kindly agreed to be my best man. I couldn't have wished for a more stalwart assistant on my big day.

Luck was with us on our Wedding Day; the sun shone from a cloudless sky, and it was a very happy occasion for both our families. The Rev. Stonham officiated, a personal friend of the Day family, with whom we kept in touch for many years, and he did in fact christen all our children, travelling specially to London Road Methodist Church, Newbury, for each occasion.

Sneaking a sly glance as my bride-to-be walked slowly down the aisle on her father's arm. The Bridal March Andante from Violin Concerto in E Minor by Mendelsohn was played on the organ. Peggy looked radiant. Was this really the sun-tanned, windswept land-girl from the poultry farm?

We smiled happily at each other as she came alongside, and we took the next few steps together, this was our day, we only had thoughts for each other.

The first hymn: "Praise my soul, the King of Heaven" was followed by the marriage ceremony. Then Psalm LXVII.

Peggy was a Sunday School teacher. The children thought the word of her, they asked if they could sing 'Morning Star Hymn' for a very special teacher.

After the address, which was quite moving, we sung the final hymn "Love Divine, all loves excelling."

A reception for a limited number of guests was held at the Upcross Hotel, Berkeley Avenue, Reading. Limited not only on numbers to be invited, but on the menu itself. Food was strictly rationed, but our families had given some of their coupons to the caterers, so that they could put on a few extra luxuries. Nervously I got up and said a few words. The bride's father, the best man and a favourite uncle did the same. Rather a quiet affair, and by five o'clock Peggy had changed into her very smart 'going away' outfit, a pretty pink floral summer dress, which showed off her slim figure to perfection.

We lost little time in getting away, there had been some hanky-panky to my Vauxhall Saloon, but nothing serious. Soon we were on our way at last. What a relief, that final escape to freedom, just the two of us, after the planning and tension of the last few days. Paignton, Devon, here we come, but my car wouldn't make that distance on post war-time roads before night-fall. We spent our wedding night at the Ship Hotel, Mere, in Somerset.

Two glorious weeks on the South Devon coast followed. I had never had such a long holiday, and the weather was beautiful, but then I expect it always is on a honeymoon!

The intimate details here have been censored!!!

Ours was to be a very happy marriage, based on true love, we never quarrelled, and rarely had a cross word. It lasted for the next thirty years ending abruptly with the tragic and untimely death of my dear wife at the age of 54.

Back to the Grindstone

Two glorious weeks by the sea, then back to work. I had to support a wife now, and no one paid me to be on holiday!

We were now hand-milking two dairy herds, running both farms as one, under the title of F. Houghton & Son, my father and mother owning a 50% share between them; my sister Delcie and myself 25% each, although it must be remembered that I had paid for all the live and dead stock on Mousefield Farm on taking it over from the previous tenant, Mr Eli Cross. Dad and Delcie were milking between 16 to 20, mainly shorthorn, cows, in the old, galvanised tin cladded cowshed at Dymond Farm.

My Channel Island herd at Mousefield was down to twelve, but they were all first rate cows, some giving over five gallons per day, and all over 5% butter fat. It must be remembered that they were fed during the winter months on home produced feed. Best hay, plus rolled barley, chopped swedes or mangolds. Mangolds grew well on the farm's deep sandy loam. Dunged heavily in the Autumn, planted the following April, we grew mangolds up to twelve inches in diameter, and weighing twenty-eight pounds. Supposed to be 90% water, nevertheless, the cows liked them. They were good grub, filling the hungry gap in early Spring before turn-out time. Marrow stem kale was another of our Winter standbys. This was cut with a hand slasher and transported every day to the cow stall, by horse drawn wagon. A hand freezing, thankless task on cold winter mornings.

My Guernsey cows came in for the Winter about the end of October, depending on weather conditions. Once brought in they stayed under cover until Spring turn out. They had bowls in front of them, the water flow being activated by the cow pressing down a small metal plate with her nose. A chain around each cow's neck kept each animal in its rightful place, yet allowed a limited amount of movement. Mucking out was quite a chore, we bedded them down daily with fresh clean straw, but unless one checked round two or three times during the day, and last thing at night, to move the dung pats back into the gutter, you had cows with very filthy udders next morning!!

My 'town-bred' wife of a few days set to with enthusiasm. Our working day commenced at 6 am, with our twelve cows. Entering the cowshed, somewhat bleary eyed, our row of fawn and white gold-top milk producers were placidly chewing the cud, with full stomach, they groaned and grunted loudly, rising reluctantly, hind quarters first. Stretching themselves, each one now presented us with almost half a wheel-barrow full of fresh cow-dung. "Careful, now, as you walk behind them, it was not unknown for one to cough at an inappropriate moment, expelling the strong smelling material into the open tops of the cowman's wellies!"

Peggy was completely 'green' when it came to handling bovine animals, but she was determined she was going to learn to milk. "Come on, show me what to do!" she demanded. "Well, like this" I say, giving the first cow a gentle push to make her 'set' her leg. Perching my backside on the edge of the three-legged stool, bucket held between my knees, head tucked well into the cows flank, I commence to draw a full stream of rich, creamy milk with each squeeze of well accomplished hands. Swish, swish, swish, the milk rose quickly in the bottom of the four gallon purpose built dairy bucket. This was 'Guttsy', she let her milk down well, providing she had a trough full of bait under her nose. Soon there was two inches of white froth rising quickly in the pail.

Rising from the stool, I emptied my bucket, handing over to my land girl wife. To watch an old hand milk a cow, it looks so easy, but so frustrating for a beginner to squeeze and pull with such little results. My wife was getting cross: "Why can you do it, and I can't, what am I doing wrong?" "Patience, my dear, patience" I replied, "practice on the same cow twice a day for a week, and by then you'll milk a cow faster than I can." Sure enough, she did just that. I must admit I never learnt her skills in dress-making or ever became useful in the kitchen!

My father usually had a bull running with the herd. Providing it was a good 'worker' he was not too interested in the breed, or what cross it was. There were regulations that stated: "Bulls had to be pure bred, of good confirmation and true to type" – a licence was to be obtained for each young bull on reaching nine months of age. Dad ignored this law!

It wasn't easy getting my Guernsey cows in calf, difficult at times to detect when they were 'in season' since they were tied up all through the winter months. If I thought one was 'bulling', the bull was led up the road to Mousefield with a bull stick fastened to the brass ring in the bull's nostrils, then the cow was let out into the yard for service.

Dad was willing to let nature take its course with his cows. They got in calf, if and when they felt like it. Sometimes he milked a cow for two years, and if she failed to have a calf, it was only when her milk yield dropped to three or four pints that he packed her off for meat.

My intention was to run my dairy herd with greater efficiency. Calve them in less than 365 days, record their yields and butter fat. Cull for infertility. Of the sixteen dairy cows I had purchased from the outgoing tenant at an average price of £24 each; two had been sold barren at £11-5-0 each, another for £9 and one suffering from John's disease for £5-18-0. This debilitating illness causes the stricken animal to continually scour, and finally waste away to skin and bones. She was so thin we called her 'Rasher'. The little drop of milk this cow was giving was certain to be affected with tuberculosis bacillus, and not fit to drink. It was to be some years before our herd became 'attested'.

That first Autumn I cut the overgrown garden hedge down to size. Our sheltered, old fashioned country garden had stood neglected for three years. Weeds had taken possession. We had a good supply of well-rotted farmyard manure, I dug in two wagon loads. The soil is a rich deep loam capable of growing almost every type of vegetable. It must have been cultivated for centuries, I'm always finding broken sections of clay pipes discarded by their long dead owners.

A routine quickly developed, we worked hard, but enjoyed to the full our daily tasks, milked the cows, and fed the young stock. There was plenty of Autumn field work to do. Although by now I had my Fordson Tractor 'Teddy' the two lovely Shire horses which I had purchased from Mr Cross for £52 were worked most days in shafts. Carting mangolds, kale, hay or dung. Wet days or dry, come snow or frost, they were always willing. Which was more than could be said for my T.V.O. tractor with oiled up plugs!!

Peggy made jam, bottled fruit, cleaned the house, washed and mended dirty farm clothes, helped milk, loaded up dung, groomed the horses, did the weekly shopping, straightened out the book-keeping and still found time to go to Church on Sunday!

Farming at Mousefield – Early Post War Years

Having taken over the tenancy of Mousefield Farm I was now a farmer in my own right. The previous tenant Mr Eli Cross gave possession on Michaelmas Day 1946. The rent, £150 per annum was paid in two instalments on March 25th and September 29th.

Peggy and I could not cope with all the work involved. I placed a small advert in the Newbury Weekly News. 'Stockman or girl required to assist with milking and calf rearing' Miss Dora Jerome seemed the most suitable applicant. A farmer's daughter she had spent the war years as a Land Army girl on the dairy farm run by Mr & Mrs Gathorne-Hardy at Donnington Priory. Dora was hired. She was not put off by the fact that she would have to be at the farm by six am, in time for the morning milking. In those day she had rented accommodation in town cycling out to the farm before dawn, bringing a packed lunch with her. We were hand milking in those days. Dora did her share of the morning milking, fed the calves, helped on the farm during the day with any jobs that were going, milked again in the afternoon, leaving the farm around six o'clock to cycle home again. Seven days each week, except for every other Sunday off.

No overtime pay, just a flat rate of £2-5-0 per week. A tough life, especially during the rain and snow of winter, cycling to and fro, the faint glow of a carbon lamp piercing the darkness.

Dora was to become a symbol of Mousefield, working for the family for thirty-seven years, until her retirement on March 18th 1984. Through the whole of that period she was never once late for work, even though sometimes she had to walk, if roads were snow or ice covered. I suppose I could count on one hand the days she had off sick.

One morning with the chores completed, over our usual large breakfast of bacon and two eggs, my young wife said: "I'd like to keep a few hens, have our own eggs, so much better than those we get from the shop, and it will save on the housekeeping too!" "Thought you had had enough of poultry after five years with ole Simpson." I replied. "Oh just a dozen or so, you get me two broody hens, and I will go and talk nicely to 'Simmy', hopefully he will give me two settings of fertile eggs for my war effort."

I set to work making two hen coops. Peggy got her eggs, I purchased two 'sitty' hens. Three weeks later we had twenty-three Sussex Cross Rhode Island red chicks. They grew quickly, the two proud mothers clucking and scratching round the farm manure heaps and to a great extent finding their own food. Five/six months later our new pullets laid their first eggs and from then on we became self supporting in eggs and poultry meat.

The new enterprise expanded rapidly, and within two years my wife had some five hundred layers, all on free range. I had managed to purchase some second-hand poultry houses at local farm auction sales, mostly in need of major repairs, but a few planks of sawn timber, a new felt roof and a coat of creosote soon gave them a new lease of life.

We had expanded in line with local demand and all our eggs were sold at the door or to nearby shops. We didn't seem to be troubled with foxes at that time but years later they did get destructive.

We took no holidays in those early days, the farm demanded all our time and energy, we were certainly not getting rich but we paid our way.

Col. Walker our landlord seemed pleased with his new tenants, calling unexpectedly two or three times throughout the year for a chat and to look over his property. He kept the house and buildings in reasonable repair, but was quick to notice if the hedges were not trimmed on time or noxious weeds flourished in the pastures.

Our ageing tractor did most of the cultivations, but I still worked the two cart horses which I had taken over with the farm, chain harrow, rolling and horse hoeing the roots. From October onwards we cut a load of kale each day for the dairy herd. This was a bitterly cold job on frosty mornings. Grasping a stiffly frozen three foot high stalk of marrowstem with one hand whilst slashing it down with sickle or bill-hook, stacking it in small heaps to load later on the horse drawn wagon. More often than not the field was wet with Autumn rains, tracks a foot deep were left behind as our willing horse threw its ton weight into the collar, moving the load out to a dry part of the meadow where, standing atop the load I'd fork out the day's feed of kale in a long line as the unattended horse plodded slowly forward.

By mid-November, unless it was an exceptionally mild winter, our cows would be in at night and by Christmas would be housed completely until Spring turn-out. This meant much more work, bedding down and mucking out. By the turn of the year kale was usually finished, now I'd supplement their rations with mangolds or swedes put through the hand turned root pulper, and mixed with crushed grain or perhaps purchased sugar-beet pulp.

In the early 1950's, some foods were still on ration. Farmers were urged on by Government policy to produce more. Grants of £7-10-0 per acre were given to plough up old pasture or leys that had been down to grass for four years or more. I liked to take advantage of these payments working the plough around the farm.

If we got thirty hundred weight of wheat to the acre we reckoned we had done well. Weeds could be a problem especially thistles. We chopped off as many as we could in early Summer, going through the crop with a dutch hoe. However, the survivors were a nuisance in the sheaves at harvest time.

This was farm life at Mousefield in the early days of my farming career. We worked hard with little time for leisure activities. The seasons followed each other in rapid succession. The main thing was that we were happy in what we were doing. It was our chosen way of life.

Progress

After we stopped building hay ricks in 1952, New Bros, local corn and seed merchants came in the summer months and baled our hay with a stationery baler using wire ties. The stationery baler was a cumbersome machine but very labour saving, compared with rick building, and of course much more convenient to have bales stacked in the barn for winter feeding, even so it still required five or six men to operate it efficiently. The foreman who was also the tractor driver did little more than set up and keep his machinery in working order. Two men on the baler, one moved the heavy metal needles every time a bale was completed, threaded wires through, the man on the other side passed the wires back, and the first man twisted the end through the wire loop joining the two ends together. Bales left the chamber like a string of sausages pushed out by the great ram, thumping away, darting backwards and forwards on four small wheels. Another man stacked the bales. Real heavy weights compared to today's pick-up-bales. You didn't get many more than twenty to the ton! The farmer's job, was to pitch the swept in hay, up and into the bale hopper. Strong, sun-tanned, hairy fore-arms protruded from turned up shirt sleeves, skillfully turned a long hay fork in a good pitch of hay to continually feed the hungry monster: Whoomp – whoomp – whoomp. More, more, always demanding more. Sweat ran down Dad's face and dripped from his red nose, as he strove to get his money's worth from these hired men and machinery.

One of my jobs was to sweep the hay to the baler using a large ten tined wooden hay sweep, fastened to the front of a Rover car! The last meadow this method was used, was in fourteen acres at Mouse-field Farm in 1956.

The next labour saving device in the hay-field was the pick-up baler. A machine that picked up hay from windrows, rammed it tight into oblong bales, tied baler twine around each bale, and ejected neatly to a man riding a wooden sledge behind. One had to be very sure footed to ride this bucking, swaying platform and at the same time stack five to eight hay bales whilst on the move, and by holding the bales with both hands, release an iron bolt with your foot, which, in turn, caused the platform to tip, and off slid your carefully stacked hay bales, and so did you, if you failed to retain your balance. The times I fell off the bloody thing was nobody's business. On regaining your balance, you had to turn, run, then jump on again before the driver vanished over the brow of the next hill. He couldn't care less what was happening at his rear!

Our first pick-up baler, a red painted Massey, was a massive affair. 'Teddy', my faithful Standard Fordson, put all his four champion plugs to full use, as he struggled to drag this reluctant piece of heavy machinery round and round the field. On up hill stretches foul black smoke from the exhaust blacked out the sun. This baler boasted its own petrol engine to drive the 'works'. A great metal arm with large jagged teeth swung up and down in an erratic fashion, pushing the seasoned grass into the baling chamber. The two knotters, a law unto themselves, were best left well alone, they just seemed to have good days and bad!

Not until we purchased a tractor with P.T.O. (power take-off) could we invest in a pick-up-baler without the necessity of having its own motor power. We had our fair share of eager young reps only too anxious to part us from our hard earned money. "Bamfords have turned out a good baler, Dad, we should get one. Two or three of those farmers up the Lambourn Valley have bought one, get our hay baled twice as quick." "That's the Liddiard's and the like, pots of money them lot got, our old un 'll do us a few more seasons yet!" Dad replied. I won the day, we bought a green painted Bamford for £960, an unheard of sum to spend on machinery. "That son of yours will break us if he goes on like that, Frank. If it goes wrong you can't put it right neither," said my mother.

It didn't go wrong, and not only did I bale up our own hay in half the time it took previously, but baled a few thousands for neighbours too! We still dragged the small wooden sledge behind and it was to be a few seasons later that we purchased an automatic metal sledge, with the rear gate operated from the tractor seat by means of a long cord, thus dispensing with tail end Charlie (an R.A.F. expression for the rear gunner). One could now drop off eight or ten bales to be stacked up later. That was another laborious, back-aching job, as there was always a desperate rush to get them all stood up before it rained. Even then the bales were not much more than shower proof. A wet day or heavy thunderstorms soon spoilt well made hay. This little Bamford baler did us well for eight or nine summers, but by the time my son, Tim, started using it, it was beginning to forget how to tie knots, despite being well maintained, always checked over at the end of season and stored away for the winter, clean, greased and oiled. Its very frustrating on one's nerves to use a machine that for no apparent reason throws out a long line of broken bales!

Now, its my turn to be told what is required in the hay and harvest field. "A Welger, that's what we want Dad." "Got a lot greater capacity" says son Tim. "Well, perhaps he's right." I admit to myself. We do a part exchange deal. Our new Welger AP12 turned out to be a wonderful baler. This was followed in due course by the Welger AP52, an even better machine.

Next came our present baler, a John Deere which set the farm account back some £7,500. This machine ties round bales, hay, straw or silage. Its even got electronic devices which cause red lights to flash in the air conditioned tractor cab which keeps the operator informed on progress at the rear.

In the old days, making bales was one thing, getting them into the barn another! 'If hay is fit to bale its fit to stack' – so the saying goes. However, our hay, carted from the field by tractor and trailer was stacked in the great old barn at Mousefield. This ancient traditional timber and tiled roofed building was originally built to store sheaves of corn to be threshed out in winter by hand flail. Each summer, if we had had a good hay harvest, the bales would be stacked to the very top of the barn. Way up amongst the massive oak beams, spiders and our resident bats.

To get the last bales right to the apex, we swung them up by ropes on block and tackle. What a laborious task that was, one bale at a time, and golly, didn't we sweat on hot summer days, there was just no air up there, under the roof tiles.

We dare not fill the barn too quickly, just put a load or two in each day. Giving each layer of hay time to sweat out a little. Fire was always a danger. To allow air to circulate freely between the stacked bales we left some narrow tunnels, this was a great help to dry the sap from new made hay. Unfortunately, it gave lovely nesting places for our free range hens. We found a large proportion of these eggs whilst still fresh, but many remained hidden until finally discovered in spring as our store of hay finally vanished into hungry cows' stomach's. The farm-yard boasted two or three fine mature roosters, who always did their stuff, and there are few more satisfactory sights than a proud mother hen appearing one spring morning with her brood of multi-coloured chicks.

Ten, maybe fifteen years ago, I would have said that hay baling and the transport of the bales couldn't progress any further. How wrong I was!

Today in the mid 1980's, bales, and big round ones at that, are moved from meadow to livestock use untouched by hand! We had an intermediate stage using a conventional baler and a MacConnel bale packer, one of the few ever used in this area. An unwieldy piece of machinery costing us some £5,000. Nevertheless, tagging along behind the baler it gobbled up hay or straw bales by the thousand, and in a mystic arrangement of levers, springs, wheels and heavy duty baler twine usually, but not always, managed to tie a pack of twenty bales. The whole ponderous outfit moving slowly round the field, occasionally parturition occurred rather like an elephant giving birth!

These days we don't make hay, my sons can't cope with the fickleness of the English climate. We baled and wrapped silage for the first time last season i.e. 1986. Excellent job. Round straw bales are stacked outside pyramid fashion. The round bales shed rain like feathers on a duck's back, and these are moved two at a time on steel spikes fitted to a tractor foreloader as and when required.

From Farming Tenant to Landowner

The mid 1950's found my wife and I with a growing family of three young sons, all potential farmers, in my mind. It was my ambition to acquire more farm land, but seldom in our little valley did any come on to the market. With no money we couldn't consider moving to another area, although on one occasion, at a much later date, we did take a trip to South Wales, looking at farms for sale in the Carmarthen area, and actually made an offer of £24,000 for a large rundown dairy farm. Secretly, I was pleased we didn't get it.

We did rent the odd parcel of summer grazing here and there, but that was usually more trouble than it was worth, either there was no water readily available, or the fences were in a bad state of repair. Cattle put in to graze always seem to get out into someone's garden after dark, or early on Sunday morning!

Then one day, the morning mail brought a letter from A.W. Neate & Sons, local agent and auctioneers in Cheap Street, Newbury. Wilfred Rowles of Highwood Farm, had decided to put Red Farm on the market. Ninety acres, a range of traditional brick and tile farm buildings, and two cottages. The letter explained that prior to being auctioned, the farm was being offered privately to the three immediate neighbours. The price required was ten thousand pounds.

This was indeed a golden opportunity, so rarely did adjoining land come up for sale. It would fit in well with our two existing small holdings, giving us something over 250 acres. If I got it, I would be joining the 'big farmer class'. The snag was where was I going to find £10,000. My father made it clear that he wasn't interested in expansion at his time of life, with the prospect of getting into debt. Neither could I ignore the opposition. Captain J.S. Fairhurst, on the western boundary, Mr and Mrs M.A. Colefax on the northern. Both these prospective purchasers had of course received details of the property, and I was positive that they would be quickly putting in their offers. I couldn't compete with my wealthy neighbours.

"You may as well forget about buying that farm," said my wife. "Getting sleepless nights over it, you can't afford a new pair of trousers, so I don't see where you think you are going to get the money to buy a hundred acre farm, and you would still have to stock it afterwards." She was quite right of course, but then I have a dogged, determined nature once I set my heart on something. I figured that by selling off some livestock, and scraping up every penny I had, I might just get two thousand pounds together. Dad relented and said he would loan me a thousand pounds. I'd have to try my bank manager for the remainder, but the problem was I owned no land being only a small tenant farmer with a large family.

Days, weeks passed by. One morning over breakfast, Peggy said. "I've changed my mind over Red Farm, I've got a feeling we are going to get it, its no good giving up yet, why don't you go into Newbury, and make the agents an offer for it?"

The car refused to start, I really would have to buy a new battery. I cycled into town, lean my bike against a wall, and bolding marched into Neate's office. The receptionist, a rather stern, middle aged lady, greeted me with the words. "Can I help you, Sir?" "I wish to see Mr Frank Neate." I replied. "He is with a client, if you care to take a seat, I'll see if he can see you when he is free, may I enquire the nature of your business?" "I have received a letter from him concerning the sale of a farm, and I wish to discuss details." I replied.

It looked like being a long wait, I picked up an outdated copy of 'Country Life', flicking through pages advertising expensive properties, antique auction sales, articles on hunting, fishing, and other country pursuits. I would have to consider joining the Country Landowners Association if I bought this farm.

A portly, well dressed gentleman emerged from a side door, bid the receptionist a pleasant good-day and left.

Minutes later: "Mr Neate will see you now, Sir, if you will kindly come this way." The firms senior partner rose from behind an antiquated mahogany desk, we shook hands. "Please take a seat Mr Houghton, you've called to discuss the sale of Red Farm I gather?" Without waiting for a reply he continued in his articulate manner. "Nice block of fertile land, its a useful farm, just do you. I understand you have young sons, they will want to farm later on, no doubt?"

Handing over an O.S. sheet he continued: "The land for sale is coloured pink with a blue mark on the boundary. You'll notice its all within a ring fence, also it has a long road frontage. There is mains water to the buildings and cottages but no electricity, of course."

He paused for a moment, looked inquiringly across his desk and said: "You in the running, young man? We are open to offers of course, but I doubt if my client will be willing to cut his price."

There is an old saying: "If you don't shoot you'll not kill." With more bravado than hope I said. "I'll go to six thousand pounds if that is any good." He was silent for a moment before replying. "I know my client will not consider that figure, but we will keep in touch, if there is any new developments or if you wish to increase your offer don't hesitate to contact me again."

Out in the street my cycle stood where I had left it. Downcast I peddled home. Peggy was busy in the dark, dreary box like room that served as a kitchen. "Put the kettle on love, let's have a cup of tea, there's little chance of us buying Red Farm with our kind of money." With a smile of encouragement my wife said. "Oh, come on, not like you to give up, we will win in the end, you'll see." "I'll go and see Wilfred myself."

Days drifted into weeks, rumour had it that the farm had already been sold. Over the grapevine I heard that Jim Fairhurst didn't wish to extend his estate over into our valley. I decided it would be prudent to visit the other would-be purchasers namely Mr & Mrs Colefax.

Invited into their drawing-room, over a glass of excellent sherry, I stated the purpose of my visit.

"If you are buying the land next door, would you consider selling me 20 or 30 acres, it would be a great asset to my family if we had a few more fields?"

Their answer was a surprise. "We are not making an offer, you see we are not particularly interested in the property, as you know its a very run down place and the two cottages are condemned, quite a liability in fact, you go ahead and buy it, we wish you luck."

A few days later, returning from the school run, Peggy bumped into Wilfred at Shaw Post Ofice. Back at the farm she hurried round to the cowyard where I was mucking out.

With excitement in her voice, she said: "If you go round to Highwood Farm next Saturday morning, Wilfred will see you, he is getting anxious about selling his farm. The Newbury Council is putting pressure on him to move his wholesale butchers business out of town. He told me that he had purchased a two acre site off Pound

Lane, Thatcham, and he plans to build a new slaughter house there.

Saturday morning, I walked to Highwood across the fields. Mrs Rowles answered the door and escorted me through to the lounge. Wilfred was just stoking the log fire, he rose and we exchanged greetings.

"I've called to see you about Red Farm, was wondering if you are going to accept my offer of six thousand pounds?" I said.

"I hadn't intended to accept less than ten thousand, but I'd rather you had it than anyone else, Bert – in which case I'd accept eight thousand off you." "I'd like the farm but I just haven't got that sort of money, Wilfred."

For the next hour or so we sat and chatted about farming in general all the while the fire gave off a pleasant warmth. Flickering fingers of yellow-orange flames danced between the dry elm logs, smoke curled in lazy patterns up the chimney. Whilst outside winter still held the land in its frosty grip.

I glanced at the clock on the mantlepiece, it had turned twelve. Finally I said: "Do you think there is a possibility of us striking a deal over this land:" "Not unless you spring a bit" he replies. It was just as if we were buying and selling a cow or a litter of pigs. "Look Wilfred, we are not miles apart, try and meet me." I pleaded.

He remained silent, deep in thought. Then: "How 'bout we split the difference – seven thousand pounds."

I had a feeling that this was his final offer, no way would he drop lower in price. "Tell you what I'll do Wilfred, put in Highwood field (an extra seventeen acres) and I will agree to your price."

"Done!" he replied. Then we shook hands on the deal. Just like that!!

Red Farm, Shaw, Newbury 106.329 acres. Two cottages and buildings for the sum of seven thousand pounds. Documents signed on the 2.4.1957.

Two years later on 29.9.1959 I purchased Mousefield Farm for the sum of £4,100 from the Landlord, Lt.Col. P.M. Walker, of West Street Farmhouse, Burghclere, Newbury.

Through age and ill-health he was moving to a nursing home, and didn't wish to retain the property.

Reclamation of Redfarm Scrubland

When I purchased Red Farm from Wilfred Rowles in 1957 the twenty acres of downland had reverted to the wild. Just a tangled mass of unchecked brambles, black thorn and other small trees up to twenty feet in height. Where there was still open ground little grass remained, having long been overpowered by thistles, ragwort and rushes. The soil, heavy clay over sandy subsoil being on quite a steep slope caused the land to slip or run like molten lava in a wet winter. This land had been cultivated in the distant past, there is strong evidence of terrace farming running north-south. The boundary fence with the Fairhurst estate was almost non-existent and followed a dog-leg course. I approached Jimmy Fairhurst through his agent. "Would he agree to sell a small parcel of land?" I inquired. I could then straighten the line of our boundary, erect and maintain a stock-proof fence to the benefit of both parties.

Replying that his client didn't normally sell land, however, in this case, he would make an exception and agree to my proposal. We were both to accept the valuation of an independent valuer. The new boundary was pegged out. On measurements being taken I would be purchasing something in excess of half an acre. The new fence would be of creosoted pine – three – four inch tops. Six feet between posts, five strands of barbed wire with strainers every fifty yeards. The fence I eventually erected is still there today and has needed practically no repairs to it. The valuation put on this land by Mr F.W. Neate was £15.0.0. The fee of two guineas was shared equally between myself and the vendor.

The new fence was a smart affair, marking clearly the boundary line between our two estates.

We now had to tackle fifty years of neglect. I required a contractor with a bull-dozer and a fearless driver as the slope of the land was dreadfully steep in places. Pettit-Mills of Hyde-End Farm, Brimpton came and gave a quote for the job. Despite the fact that he had an artificial leg he walked the rough terrain with ease.

The price for the 250 horse power dozer including driver and fuel was thirty shillings per hour. 'Eric' the driver working eight hours per day, six days a week, cleared the land in just under five weeks. At the top of the hill mainly in the section purchased from Fairhurst, pollard ash and gnarled oak trees were too big and tough rooted to be moved by machinery. Eric, an expert in the use of explosives blew the old stumps out of the ground. High on this downland field is a small valley which is reached before the final summit marking the highest point of all the land we farm.

To clear, burn and leave the land workable took 221 hours of bull-dozer time for the cost of £332.15.0.

To farm my additional land I required another tractor. One Thursday after market my father and I called at the showroom of Martin & Chillingsworth in London Road, Newbury. "Yes" the agent said, "we will be only too pleased to demonstrate what the Massey Ferguson TE20 can tackle. I'll send my fitter out tomorrow if you wish Mr Houghton." "The land we want to plough has just been reclaimed, its rugged, heavy clay with quite a gradient." I explained. "No problem, these tractors will tackle anything. We will fit steel wheels and attach a mounted semi-digger two furrow plough. She'll stop at nothing, you'll see." Sure enough, next morning this diminutive tractor was unloaded, fueled and ready, it looks most unlikely to be able to successfully tackle this truly mammoth task. The weather had deteriorated in the night, but after early morning rain the sun came out between scurrying clouds and there was a drying wind. "This the bit of ground you want ploughed, governor?" asked the driver apparently undismayed by the steepness of the ground. We marked out with three flags in line (just a piece of white cloth tied to a hazel stick). I was positive in my own mind that no way was this little grey toy of a tractor going to climb the hill, let alone turn over two furrows on the way to the top!! The driver dropped the plough, opened up the throttle, and away he went. The Fergie made it to the top, but only by easing the plough on the hydraulics on the heavy clay sections.

Following this demonstration I purchased the tractor and plough. The price £525. "Betsy" we called her and she did thousands of hours of work on our farms in the next 25 years.

Alec Adnams first came to work on my farm in the school holidays, weekends and evenings. At this time if he came into our farm kitchen and sat on a chair his feet did not touch the floor, he was that small. By the time he left my employment he was into his thirties and weighed almost twenty stone! He had recently left school and was about fifteen years old when he ploughed Red Farm Hill with the new Fergie. In the end it had to be ploughed down hill. This was time consuming, but it was the only way. Today we have four wheeled drive John Deere tractors. Even those giant machines would find the hill with its heavy clay soil quite a challenge pulling their five furrow reversibles!!

Following the plough with a light set of disc harrows I bumped and tossed over rock hard clods of clay on the hard iron seat of my old Standard Fordson, trying desperately to get a reasonable seedbed. Next, field harrows criss-cross the land dragging to the surface trailer loads of broken tree roots. I grew two successive crops of spring barley (Procter). The yield was about average for our area (25 or 26 cwts to the acre). To cultivate the Hill was hard, tough work on men, tractor and combine, and it was amazing that we didn't tip over on such a gradient. No roll-bars on the tractors in those days! I was paid the government grant of £12 per acre to plough up extremely difficult land. Those were the days when farmers were being encouraged to grow the maximum from every acre. "Food from our own resources" was the slogan of the day!

Today visitors seem to doubt my word when I tell them that I drove a Massey bagger combine on the hill at Red Farm.

The second crop of spring barley was undersown with grass seed, permanent pasture at the rate of 30 lbs. to the acre. This twenty acre field also received three tons of Fison's granular concentrated compound fertiliser. Price delivered to farm £26.17.6 per ton. Now that I farmed two hundred and fifty acres I felt justified in making a much larger purchase of fertiliser, hence the fact that my order was for a six ton load!

It would seem to be rather rash of me to blow half the load on one field, the rest of the farm certainly received a very thin dressing but that is what my old diaries state!

The Ministry of Agriculture paid a subsidy of £6.3.9. this to encourage farmers to use more fertiliser. The amount of subsidy varied according to nitrogen content.

At this time I didn't own a combined drill; the last word in grain farming whereby fertiliser and seed is drilled into the seed-bed by the same spout: we still had to make two passes over our ground at seeding time. One to broadcast fertliser by means of a small box

172

spreader, nine feet wide which sprinkled out the granulated artificial by means of rotating star wheels, and two, the seed with our fifteen coulter disc drill.

There was only one way to broadcast grass seed. With our shandy barrow. The three sided box fourteen feet wide, is attached to a wheel-barrow like frame. A single large wooden spoked wheel with an inner ring of cogs which engaged a cog-wheel in the box turning the long thin shaft on which at set intervals was a series of circular brushes. Pushing your shandy barrow over land recently flattened by a Cambridge roller these same brushes flicked out the seed through a small circular hole which could be adjusted down to half-moon size according to the rate of seed required per acre.

On a flat field it is possible to seed ten or twelve acres per day, but on Red Farm Hill the steep slope meant that if one attempted to cross the gradient one side of the box touched the ground whilst the opposite side was some five or six feet in the air. On the low side the seed didn't have time to fan out and on the other even a gentle breeze caused the seed to blow in all directions.

It had to be up and down if I was going to plant my grass seed.

Edna Peel, a country lass of sixteen, just out of my old school in Love Lane, had entered my employ. From old redundant horse harness I fashioned a set of shoulder harness to fit Edna. Some traces made from plough lines attached to the front of the shandy barrow completed the job. We were away. I pushed and steered for the marker flags, Edna leaning forward, put her young shoulders to the task.

That was how Red Farm downs was re-seeded. It's been a good pasture ever since and will still fatten a summer bullock without any additional feed!

Just Mud

I have always envied those spotlessly clean grain farms with their acres of sweep concrete yards and not a thing out of its allotted place, If they have a few superior Charolais beef steers yarded in two foot depth of best wheat straw the mud left behind by the feed tractor is scraped up every day.

With our large dairy herd and all the followers things are just not like that on our farm.

Mud: Every winter and most summers too, we have vast quantities of the stuff. It is made by mixing together rain water, soil and cow dung in equal parts. Stir with tractor, trailer, milk and feed lorry wheels to a consistency of black custard. The steady procession of reps trying to sell 'new' products or calling with little hope of getting a cheque on some outstanding account, all do their bit. Even cows feet will do an excellent job in the right weather. Hot sun and strong warm winds can destroy the mixture completely, causing it to evaporate and blow away as dust.

Snow is a useful addition and definitely adds a certain amount of new colour to this otherwise rather drab material.

Last year 1985 we were in the fortunate position of having a great surplus of this unpleasant, slimy, liquid substance, so we let it filter across the meadow into a large murky pond and thence to overflow onto the main road, where it was collected on the wheels and underparts of passing vehicles, and distributed to all parts of the country. There were numerous complaints from some motorists, who said that they "didn't wish to receive these free samples."

They were so annoyed in fact, that they called in the local police, who promptly erected large warning notices, saying: "SLOW MUD ON ROAD".

They even threatened me with fines or imprisonment if I didn't stop this atrocious practice. Now, that would have been a great solution – I would have been out of the way in a nice clean cell, well away from this awful quagmire, and they could have cleaned it up themselves. Ha! Ha!

Instead we contributed to the cost of laying a large drain under the B4009 thus moving the problem to our land on the other side which had previously been dry!

Rearing a Family

My new bride stated she hoped to have six babies, being an only child she had longed for brothers and sisters. Some two years previous I had proudly taken my new girl friend to tea at my Grandparents home. Grandma Perris had cast a keen eye over my choice, whilst we all sat round a small table in the sitting room, drinking tea from the best china, with homemade scones, cream and strawberry jam.

Grandad proclaimed that Peggy as a strong outdoor girl, would make a good farmer's wife, and, in his outspoken way, forecast we should have six children. The only way to get cheap, reliable labour on a farm is to rear your own, he stated with some authority.

We had not been back many weeks from our honeymoon in Devon when Peggy started to suffer from 'morning sickness'. "You can't be having a baby yet, would never happen so quick as that, would it dear?" "I'm not so sure of that" my new wife said. "I reckon we spent more time in bed than we did on the beach! I shall make an appointment to see Dr Hett this week."

Two days later we drove to town, I sat outside in the car, calmly reading the morning paper quite convinced it was just a false alarm. Peggy came out from the Surgery, I remember she had a happy smile on her face. Getting into the passenger seat she slapped my leg: "Come on, take me home, you'll have to milk your own cows from now on, you are going to be a dad!" This was marvellous news, but I must say I was a bit shattered. My wife pregnant, "Goodness me! How quickly it had all happened. This was a new problem!"

Soon there was a mad rush to get the nursery ready, till now we hadn't even decided which room we would use, at least we had a big house with five bedrooms so we wouldn't, at least, be under any pressure for space. At first we kept our secret, in case it was a false diagnosis. But it soon came out that Peggy was visiting the doctor. Both sets of parents were delighted with our news, it would be the first grandchild on both sides and also a first great grand-child for my grandparents on my mother's side of the family.

It wasn't long before the ladies got busy knitting. We purchased a new pram, navy blue on four high spoked wheels, beautifully sprung, it was to go great service until it ended its days as a go-cart! The cot was second-hand, and even in those days a rather old-fashioned, high-sided wooden affair.

It is amazing how much advice one gets from well-meaning parents. Various quaint suggestions to relieve morning sickness which had no effect whatever. "No, you shouldn't buy a pram, a cot, bedding or anything like that yet, it might bring bad-luck, the baby could be still-born or something wrong with it." 'Poppycock!" we both agreed.

July 27th 1947, nine months and a few days after our wedding day Michael John was born at Mousefield Farm delivered by the local midwife with the doctor arriving shortly afterwards. Michael was a fine baby, weighed 7 lbs. and had delayed his arrival until it was just 'respectable'.

Why I don't know, but it was me that seemed to receive all the congratulations. I had a son, someone to take over the farm at some future date. To a farmer a son is all important. The land is permanent, farming goes on generation after generation, and a farmer always strives to leave his land in better heart than when he took over.

Michael was a 'good' baby, he grew quickly and had few problems teething. However one cannot deny that an addition to the family does rather upset the routine. Peggy was to breast feed all her babies which certainly simplifies meal times, but they still demand attention every few hours. Getting up their wind, doesn't matter which end! Changing nappies, rows of clean washing fluttering in the summer breeze. No disposables in those days!

From a very early age, our baby was put in the pram to spend many hours in the garden. The hood up if it rained, a string net in the front to keep out our farm cats. Well wrapped up in the winter months with lots of woollies and mitts, our garden was sheltered by a high thick beech hedge, which retained its leaves even in winter. Because the lawn was on a slope the pram was tied with a piece of rope to the variegated holly tree. With so much work to do on the farm, perhaps we were guilty of leaving him for too long to play with his few toys, as he developed a habit of throwing everything out of his pram, and I mean everything – first his toys, then his gloves, his booties, all the covers, the removable floor, then, on one memorable

NOT JUST A BERKSHIRE FARMER

occasion – himself! The pram was tied to the tree, Michael was strapped in and hanging over the side, he got the straps twisted around his neck. Our precious son was ten months old, his life was saved by Dora, our recently arrived dairy-maid who had heard a faint whimpering sound whilst she was feeding the calves.

Our plans for six children were shelved. Money was desperately short. Even though we were mainly self sufficient we led a frugal life, the income from fourteen or fifteen Guernsey cows, and two or three hundred laying birds, doesn't leave a lot after feed bills are paid, also there was the rent of the farm at £75 twice a year, and my landlord, Lt. Col. Walker, expected it on the day due – not a week late!

My wife and I never used any form of contraceptive, simply relied on keeping a wary eye on the calendar. This method was successful until our next holiday. We spent ten days at Minehead on the north Somerset coast. Anthony Mark was born on the 28th April the following Spring. It is a date I well remember, it had been a late, cold spring and on that day I had planted the last field of barley in the 'fourteen acres'.

Two or three more years passed by. Peggy yearned for a daughter. Our third baby, Timothy Paul, born at Mousefield Farm, was a fine handsome child. With money a little more plentiful in our household, we had made arrangements to have a private nurse. I collected Nurse Petit from Aldworth and she was to stay at our farmhouse for one month to help in general with the new baby. In fact she was with us for four of our babies. She forecast before Tim was born that it would be another boy, stating her belief that the sexes ran in three's in a family. She was correct, of course, in our case.

One thing that sticks vividly in my mind about Tim's upbringing is that he spent more time in the 'ice box' than any of the other children. On the west side of our house was a glass porch, no windows that opened, but with two doors that were lockable. If a child was extremely naughty the punishment could be twenty minutes imprisonment, and Tim spent many a spell locked in for some serious misdemeanour. On a cold frosty morning, when perhaps not fully dressed, this usually resulted in better cooperation for a while!

We got our longed for daughter on 13th October 1957 – Jane Beverley. Her mother's pride and joy, Jane was always good. I really can't remember her ever being naughty or difficult, and she was to be a great help to her Mother a few years later assisting with the later additions to our growing family.

People have often said to me "How ever did you and your wife cope with such a crowd of youngsters?"

The fact is, older children look after the younger members, bath them, feed them, take them out for walks. Kids are smart and will use all sorts of tricks to get their own way, but they soon learn that crocodile tears get them nowhere in a large family. If one was crying or being quarrelsome without good reason, Peggy would say: "Shut that child in its bedroom until it learns how to behave." Dragged upstairs and locked in, the belligerent member of the Houghton family would stamp their feet and bellow even louder, but life continued as normal downstairs, time didn't allow for any individuals to be mollycoddled.

Richard James, our fifth child, was the last to be born at Mousefield. Richard was a 'long' baby at birth, and subsequently grew into the tallest member of the family. As a child Richard suffered from dyslexia which held him back at school. We did pay for him to have special evening reading lessons which helped him a great deal. Next in his education came a period as a 'day boy' at Prior's Court School. He then moved on to Kingswood College, Bath. Somehow we managed to pay the fees at this expensive private school. He did enjoy his schooling there and Peggy and I had some very pleasant days in the City at mid-term, and open-days. Richard cried when the time came for him to leave Kingswood. He had become quite attached to the school and his friends.

The years were passing by, one more baby would give us our target figure of six. Dare we hope for a sister for Jane? If we have another, it will definitely be our last, the last throw of the dice! Unlike some unlucky couples, babies were not difficult to produce in our household, but we had to take what came as far as their sex was concerned, like everyone else. Sure enough, baby number six was another boy! Stephen Charles, born on November 14th 1961, at Battle Hospital, Reading. It also happens to be Prince Charles' birthday on that day, so Stephen always had the National Anthem played on the early morning news bulletin of the B.B.C.! Played just for him, he used to think in his younger days.

That was the completion of our family, five boys and just the one girl, at least we had reckoned so. Two years later Peggy was pregnant once more, this was completely unplanned, a mistake if you like, after all, my wife was now forty-three years old, and another baby would be a drain on her strength and health, not to mention our finances! What's more, it was certain to be another male child. There

was a limit to the future labour force our farm could carry – we could hardly go back to cutting our corn with a binder, stooking, rick-building, milking our cows by hand or similar labour intensive methods, just to absorb the muscle power of six young men! We worried unnecessarily, there is a lot of truth in the saying: "Don't cross the bridge before you get to it."

Our seventh and last baby, arrived on April 19th 1963, a lovely little girl, all the family were delighted. Jane, then seven years old was 'over the moon', a real live sister to mother and play with. They always proved to be very close, despite the slight age gap. They were also a great comfort to each other at the time of their Mother's untimely death, when Bobby was just eleven years old.

The previous tenants of this farm, Mr and Mrs Eli Cross had reared their five children here, the Gore's before them had had quite a large family, now once again the walls of this lovely, centuries old farmhouse rang with cries and laughter of a large, happy and carefree farming family!

Holidays with the Kids

Despite a busy farm life with the tie of live-stock, we usually managed two weeks holiday during the summer school vacation.

The day to day running of the farm was left in Dora's (our dairy-maid's) capable hands, whilst in the early days my father was at hand to keep his experienced eye on things.

When Michael and Tony were young we towed our caravan to the New Forest parking in a pleasant clearing not far from Lyndhurst. A permit had to be obtained from the warden, which cost five shillings per week. As the family increased older children slept in a tent pitched nearby. We had great fun exploring the forest glades, making bows and arrows and climbing trees. The sea and beach at Mudeford was within easy reach by car. The disadvantage to this type of holiday was the preparation needed before we set off. With a large family it was almost like organising some military operation. We did try to cut down to bare necessities, even so we had to pack a change of underwear for every member, a spare set of clothes in case someone fell in the mud, or got wet, wellies, sandals, swimwear, buckets, spades, toys (which included lorries, tractors, trailers, bull-dozers, dollies and the favourite teddy) not forgetting, tennis rackets, cricket bats, wickets, balls and various inflatable rafts, rubber tyres and armbands. In a freezer pack was crammed enough fresh milk, eggs, butter and bread for the first three days. A tin opener was high on the priority list to deal with the stack of soup and baked bean tins stored aboard.

Finally, when all was packed, excitement mounting, we were ready for the off. Dora came out of her caravan to see us away. She always said the same things: "Ready at last then, got everything? Have a good time and don't worry about things back here, I'll manage al'right." "Thanks, Dora, I've locked up, you know where the key is?" I replied.

I will always remember one departure. We had checked and re-checked, everyone agreed we really had got everything. Down the farm drive, out onto the main road, I head south for the coast. We must have been all of two miles on our journey when some bright member of the family said: "Hey Dad, where's Richard?" He wasn't in the car, sure enough we had left him behind! Turning round at the next junction I drove back to the farm. Our son was still in the house, quite unconcerned. It transpired that he had made a last minute visit to the toilet as the rest of us drove off to the sea!!

All the family loved North Wales; the green valleys, rugged mountains and the long stretches of golden, sandy beaches in Tremadoc Bay.

Mrs Jessie M. Stonham – wife of the Rev. Stonham – who had married Peggy and I and later christened all our offspring – owned a real Welsh cottage at Capel Uchaf. Built of massive stones with walls two feet thick, it was constructed to withstand the wild winter gales. Snug and cosy it nestled on the side of a hill overlooking Caernarfon Bay. Behind the cottage was the sheep grazed slope of 'our mountain'. We often climbed this before breakfast, rising early to watch the sun clear the pinnacles of the Snowdon range to the east. Southward in a fertile valley lay the sleepy pattern of rural Wales, whilst beyond towered the rocky summit of Bwlch Mawr. Michael Tony and myself had ambitions to conquer this peak. Tim was only six years old, but confirmed he would be coming along too. Peggy would stay at the cottage with Jane and baby Richard.

On a clear summer morning after an early breakfast we were on our way. The dew lay heavy on the grass as we scaled 'our mountain'. We had a three mile hike in front of us before we even reached the foothills of Bwlch Mawr.

The first 1,000 feet or so was steep but not difficult. By the time we got to the rocks, Tim had tired, which meant carrying him over difficult sections. Packed in a haversack were our refreshments. A flask of cold orange drink, and some biscuits. We intended making the summit before enjoying the contents. There were no well laid out trails to follow, and roped together for safety, we were making slow progress. Like most mountain climbs everytime we reached what we felt sure was the top, still yet one more steep escarpment met our eyes. Finally, with a gasp of relief, I led my party to the rock strewn plateau.

The view was magnificent, westwards we could see Yr Eifl (The Rivals) and the long curve of Caernarfon Bay, whilst to the northeast stood the majestic peak of Snowdon 3,560 feet above sea level.

We were all elated with our 'mountaineering' success. We'd done it, climbed Bwlch Mawr, even little Tim. "Come'on Dad, let's have our drink."

I opened the haversack, only to discover it was soaking wet! The flask had broken on the climb over the rocks, all our precious orange drink was gone, and in the process had saturated all our biscuits. They were just a soggy, uneatable mess.

What a disaster! Our disappointment knew no bounds. We had all taken turns at carrying the haversack so no one could be blamed.

Faced with a long hike home it was some three hours later that four thirsty, starving, exhausted 'mountaineers' staggered up the cottage path.

These are just two of the memorable holidays we all had together.

Many happy days were spent with my sister Delcie and her husband Peter, who had moved from Shaw to farm in Devon. Over a period of some years we explored Exmoor and the rugged North Devon coast line.

Looking back I'm pleased we made the effort to spend time with our children whilst they were still young.

Beliefs

I firmly believe that one's path through this life is mapped out in advance. It can appear to be taking a set course, one which you yourself have carefully planned, only to diverge suddenly on a side-track.

1979 found me fully engrossed in running a sizeable farming unit whilst at the same time coping with the trials and tribulations of a teenage family.

I had been a widower for three years, when, through a chain of events I met the lady who was to become my second wife.

Ruth, a farmer's widow from Lancashire is one of those delightfully sunny, women who has the ability to make all who meet her feel better. After a whirlwind courtship of a few weeks, I realised I had fallen in love. Giving the subject much thought plus a few sleepless nights, I decided to propose marriage. How would I go about it? A special day and place was required. The 21st June was fast approaching, my late Father's birthday, also of course it is the longest day of the year. A date I would not forget in the future! The special place? Why not the highest point in the district – Beacon Hill.

On a beautiful Summer's evening after a stiff climb to the summit, I asked Ruth to marry me. To my delight she accepted.

A few months' later on October 6th 1979 we were married at St Mary's Church, Shaw. It turned out to be a lovely, sunny Autumn day, with our Church beautifully decorated for Harvest Festival, and almost filled to capacity with our joint family, friends and neighbours who had come to wish us well.

Now that our children have made their own way in the world, I realise how important it is to put pen to paper, and record in my own words, the vast changes that have taken place in my farming career.

In retrospect I've had a wonderful life. Mostly I've achieved all I wished to achieve, it's been interesting and varied.

I've enjoyed strength and good health, reared a family of seven children, and made friends all over the world.

It is only as I got older that I began to appreciate the dawn of every day, be it Spring, Summer, Autumn or Winter, they are all beautiful, even when it pours with rain, or the snowflakes settle silently on the lawn.

Thank you God for every one.

Stable Cottage
Red Farm
Long Lane
Newbury
Berkshire
RG16 9LE

30 November 1991

Dear Reader

I do hope you enjoy my book which, as you will discover, is based largley on my memories of my early farming years. You may be interested to learn that I have now published the sequel "Just more of the Bershire Farmer". Signed copies can be obtained for just £6.95 including p&p direct from me at the above address.

Yours Literally

Bert Houghton

Bert Houghton